Slow Cooker Magic

ALSO BY LINDA REHBERG AND LOIS CONWAY

Bread Machine Magic
More Bread Machine Magic
The Bread Machine Magic Book of Helpful Hints

A

Seasonal

Selection of

Family Favorite

Recipes

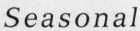

slow cooker Magic

Linda Rehberg
and Lois Conway

ST. MARTIN'S GRIFFIN ❦ NEW YORK

www.stmartins.com

Book design by Ellen Cipriano

LIBRARY OF CONGRESS CATALOGING-IN-PUBLICATION DATA
Rehberg, Linda.
    Slow cooker magic : a seasonal selection of family
favorite recipes / Linda Rehberg and Lois Conway.
        p. cm.
    Includes index (page 239).
    ISBN 0-312-32657-2
    EAN 978-0-312-32657-9
        1. Electric cookery, Slow. I. Conway, Lois. II. Title.

TX827.R43 2005
641.5'884—dc22

2005045518

10 9 8 7 6 5 4

We dedicate this book to Anita, DeDe, and Debbie,
our sisters and lifelong friends.
Nothing can ever break the bonds
that tie you to our hearts.

Linda's husband, Dennis, passed away suddenly during the editing of this book. We'd like to include him in this dedication because he touched all of our lives so deeply and was the source of much love and laughter for many wonderful years.

$\mathcal{C}$ontents ❧

Introduction ✤

OUT OF THE BREAD MACHINE, into the slow cooker. What a change for us!

As we were contemplating a fourth bread machine cookbook, we sensed a change in the air. With the emphasis on quick and easy meals these days, there's also a renewed interest in slowed-down cooking, thanks to the slow cooker. It was time to pull them out from the dark recesses of our kitchen cabinets, dust them off, and put them back to work.

We must confess that we both have husbands who groaned when informed that they'd be living on slow cooker meals for a whole year while we developed this book. But they now admit we surprised them with appetizing meals that didn't taste as if they'd been cooked to death.

Most of us work hard all day, in or outside the home, then run errands after work or madly dash from one child's after-school activity to another. By the time we walk through the front door absolutely dead on our feet, the thought of spending another hour at the stove is dreadful. No wonder the fast food industry is a multimillion-dollar business!

Enter the magic of the slow cooker. With minimal preparation the night before or first thing in the morning, you'll walk through the front door and be greeted by the smell of a hot meal ready and waiting. It's almost like having your own live-in chef! Gone, too, will be the guilt pangs over the fact that your family knows the menu of every fast food restaurant within a radius of ten miles by heart.

About Our Recipes ✄

FOR THE MOST PART, THIS book is a collection of family favorite recipes we've both used over the years, reworked to suit the slow cooker. We've included recipes you'll enjoy serving guests, but mainly these are meals you can set in front of your family without being greeted by wrinkled noses.

Yes, slow cooker meals can be healthy, light meals, too. Most of our recipes list variations that significantly reduce the fat or calories. We've also tried to walk a fine line between relying on the convenience of canned or processed foods and the health benefits of fresh foods.

We've divided this cookbook up into four seasons to make meal planning and shopping convenient. Open up the cookbook to the current season and you'll find recipes that best use what's currently fresh in your market.

We've also listed suggestions for simple side dishes that you can add to the meal in not much more time than it takes for someone to set the table. Keeping variety in your weekly menus helps reduce the tedium of cooking every day and broadens the range of foods your family—even the kids!—may learn to love. We want to make meal planning easier for you. If you can plan several entire meals ahead, you'll eliminate those daily dashes to the grocery store—a huge time saver!

For the novice, we've included cooking tips with almost every recipe, so you can learn as you go. For the experienced cook, we've listed many suggestions on ways to vary each recipe, so you can tap into your own creative instincts and use these recipes many times over without tiring of them.

And if you've opened up a chapter and nothing strikes your fancy, don't forget the Basics chapter. The Basics are the tried-and-true, everyday recipes you can always fall back on when feeling uninspired or overwhelmed by daily routines.

We tested most recipes using 4-quart Rival Crock-Pots, because it's the most popular size slow cooker. For those who own a 6-quart slow cooker, you can easily increase the recipes by tossing in more vegetables and/or a larger quantity of meat. If you need to be more precise, just multiply ingredient amounts by one and a half. Most of the recipes in this book feed four to six people.

To calculate prep times, we started the clock once we'd gathered all the ingredients together on the counter. It's a habit worth developing. Cooking is more enjoyable when everything's at hand.

So join us as we revamp much-loved family recipes, rediscover a forgotten appliance, and make old things new again!

Slow Cooker Magic

Helpful Hints

OF COURSE THE SLOW COOKER can be an everyday workhorse in your kitchen, but consider these creative uses for it: Need an extra set of hands when entertaining? The slow cooker is there for you, keeping side dishes on hold while you busy yourself with the main course. Buy a second slow cooker and you can use it for hot hors d'oeuvres or mulled beverages. We love it as a fondue pot because it holds the fondue at a perfect temperature for hours without burning the bottom. And it's wonderful on a potluck buffet table, because food will stay warm until it disappears. During the holidays, when oven space is at a premium, our slow cookers are put to good use heating up extra stuffing, keeping gravy warm, cooking bread puddings, and even for hot toddies.

If you regularly feed more than three or four people, we recommend the larger 6-quart slow cooker. You can then cook larger roasts, a whole chicken, and larger meals with the possibility of leftovers.

We also recommend the type of slow cooker that is strictly a slow cooker with heating coils that encircle the pot, not a combination deep-fryer, slow cooker, etc. with the heating element in the bottom only.

For the greatest convenience, put all the ingredients in the pot the night before, cover, and place it in the refrigerator. Then all you have to do in the morning is insert the pot into the slow cooker, plug it in, and go. For items that taste better the next day, like pasta sauce, chili, beef stew, etc., we've actually cooked them overnight, placed them in the refrigerator the next morning and then rewarmed them for dinner. The bonus of this technique is the most appetizing morning aromas.

INGREDIENTS

What the slow cooker cooks best:

Soups; stews; chilis; casseroles; beans; pasta sauce; vegetable dishes; pudding-type desserts; tough cuts of meat, like beef chuck, brisket, ribs, rump and bottom round roasts, pork shoulder, Boston butt roast, and lamb shanks.

What the slow cooker isn't well suited for:

Pieces of meat that would be better grilled quickly such as: steaks, flank steak, chops; most fish; pasta; long grain rice; dairy products such as milk, cream, and sour cream. Many times, though, you can cook them separately and add them at the end.

TIPS

If your roast doesn't quite fit into the pot, you can cut it into two pieces that will.

Dense vegetables, like carrots, are best placed on the bottom of the pot. Try to cut vegetables in similar size pieces.

In our recipes, small potatoes weigh about 4 ounces, medium potatoes are 8 ounces, large potatoes weigh between 10 and 12 ounces, and anything over that we consider jumbo potatoes.

All eggs used in these recipes are large. All butter used in these recipes is unsalted.

Try to use the freshest ingredients whenever you can. You'll be surprised at what a difference it makes.

In several recipes, rather than bouillon cubes, we've recommended a chicken, beef, or vegetable stock base, such as Better than Bouillon brand. If you can't find something similar in the soup section of your market, you can certainly substitute 1 bouillon cube for each teaspoon of stock base.

We suggest you keep a can or bottle of cooking oil spray on hand. Some of our recipes call for buttering or greasing the pot first before adding ingredients, and a quick misting of cooking oil spray is an easy way to do that.

If it's all about speed and convenience for you, don't overlook the little bags of sliced vegetables, jars of peeled garlic, frozen chopped onion, and other preprepped ingredients to make your job easier. Also, there are pre-assembled dinners designed for use in slow cookers in the markets now.

DOS AND DON'TS

For the best flavor and appearance, we strongly recommend browning meats and vegetables first in a skillet or Dutch oven on the cooktop, when the recipe calls for it. It takes a bit more time, but the payoff is worth it.

If you load up the slow cooker the night before to sit overnight in the refrigerator, do not put raw poultry in with the other ingredients. Add it to the pot just before cooking. And if you use potatoes or apples, place them on the bottom, covered with other ingredients, so they won't turn brown overnight.

If you set your slow cooker to start and stop on a timer, don't let the food sit longer than 2 hours before or after cooking, to avoid the possibility of spoiling.

Don't be tempted to lift the lid every time you pass by the cooker. Each time you peek adds another 15 minutes to the cooking time. It takes that long for the slow cooker to come back up to heat.

If you do have to lift the lid on the slow cooker to stir the ingredients, lift it straight up so that the condensation on the underside of the lid won't run back into the food.

Some slow cookers have hot spots. You'll know you have a hot spot if one particular area of the dish appears overcooked or sticks to the liner. If yours does, rotate the liner a few times during cooking to insure even cooking.

We found to our surprise that most recipes were actually done in about 4 hours on low heat; but that's not convenient for those of us who work outside the home all day. When you extend the cooking time another 4 to 6 hours to fit our working schedules, quite often the flavor is cooked right out of the food. Therefore, in many recipes we've included the recommendation to taste and reseason before serving. Also, if you sauté your dried herbs and spices in a bit of oil before using, it will help your dish retain its flavors.

Dairy products, such as milk, cream, and cheese, don't hold up during the long cooking process, but they can be added at the end. Otherwise, substitute canned evaporated milk for regular milk.

Avoid adding very strong-tasting vegetables, such as cabbage, brussels sprouts, or broccoli, to a stew. These can be cooked separately and added at the end to keep them from overpowering the dish.

RECOMMENDED ACCESSORIES

If you don't have one of the fancy new slow cookers that can be pro-
grammed to start and stop at specific times, you can still have that great
feature with the use of a household timer that turns appliances on and off at
set times. We relied on this handy little item many times and it worked just
fine. But make sure not to delay cooking for more than 2 hours on anything
that needs refrigeration.

An immersion (handheld) blender is almost a must-have item. We used
it over and over to puree sauces and soups right in the slow cooker with
ease. Trying to pour hot liquid from the slow cooker into a blender is nearly
impossible, not to mention hazardous.

We used heavy nonstick skillets quite often when browning meats and
vegetables. A regular skillet without the nonstick coating actually gets the
job done better, but you usually must compensate with a good deal more
oil. For health's sake, stick with the nonstick.

To go along with the nonstick skillet, treat yourself to a colorful, heat-
resistant rubber spatula. They come in different shapes and sizes, and we can
guarantee once you use one you'll wonder how you ever managed without it.

For certain items—such as the turkey breast—it's helpful to have either
an instant-read thermometer or a probe connected by wire to a timer/ther-
mometer to achieve the proper degree of doneness.

A whisk, a microplane grater, a good set of measuring spoons and
cups—all are items we consider essential.

Okay, an RV doesn't qualify as an accessory, but we sure think an RV
and a slow cooker are a great match. When you've settled into a spot for a
day or two, you can plug in that slow cooker and go spend the day sight-
seeing without having to worry about dinner when you return.

ADAPTING YOUR OWN
RECIPES FOR THE SLOW COOKER

Many recipes can be converted for use in your crock-pot. Here's what we
recommend:

- Avoid rice, fish, dairy products, and pasta.
- Reduce the amount of liquid in your recipe by about half.

- Season both before and after cooking, if necessary.
- Test for doneness after 4 hours, and then every hour after that.
- Most soups, stews, and casseroles take 8 hours to cook on low.
- Meat will usually be done in 6 hours.
- Poultry will usually be done in 4 hours.

MISCELLANEOUS

To prevent accidentally cracking the crockery liner, avoid extreme changes of temperature. We've caught ourselves many times dishing out meals and walking the pot over to the sink to fill it with water and let it soak during dinner. Don't do that! Chances are good when the cold water hits the hot pot, it will crack. Let it cool first; then soak it.

You *can* wash your crock-pot liner in the dishwasher. Do not use abrasive cleansers or steel wool scouring pads on the liner. Plastic scrubbing pads are okay. Avoid scratching the glazed surface with knives or sharp utensils.

If you use an extension cord, make sure it's a heavy-duty one.

Take care to keep small children away from the cooker. The outer shell on most models gets quite hot and could burn little hands.

Slow cooker temperatures:

LOW heat = 200°

HIGH heat = 300°

1 hour on HIGH heat = 2 hours on LOW heat

Avoid overfilling or underfilling the slow cooker. It should be between one-half to three-quarters full.

When pouring the heated contents of a skillet into the slow cooker pot, we suggest placing the slow cooker pot in the sink and then pouring the contents of the skillet into it. If you accidently spill the hot food, it will be easier to clean up plus you'll avoid getting burned.

To adjust any of our 4- or 4½-quart recipes for the larger 6-quart cooker, simply multiply the amounts by 1½ times and allow another hour of cooking time for larger pieces of meat. (An instant-read thermometer will help you tell if the meat is done.)

If transporting a slow cooker meal to a potluck, without a manufacturer's insulated carrier, just wrap the pot well in some newspaper and a couple of beach towels. It will stay warm for quite a while.

By the way, "Crock-Pot" is the trademark name for the slow cookers made by Rival Manufacturing Company. So, technically, not every slow cooker is a crock-pot.

The Basics

THIS SECTION IS RICH WITH old reliable recipes, the ones we prepare over and over. We think you'll return to them on a regular basis too. They defy the seasons and are delicious year round. They're simple to make, can be used in so many meal plans, and have countless variations. We've also included Monday's Vegetable Soup recipe, because it can be your secret weapon if you're on a weight-loss plan or just trying to eat healthier.

Basic Chicken Stock

Basic Beef or Veal Stock

Basic Vegetable Stock

Monday's Vegetable Soup

Simple Pasta Sauce

Lois's Pizza Sauce

Old Faithful Pot Roast

Doctored-up Pork Roast

Handy Ham

Linda's Easy Cheesy Potatoes

Basic Risotto

Bread Pudding Galore

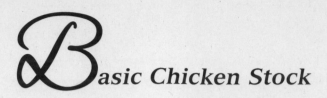

Basic Chicken Stock

This is a very simple, basic recipe for chicken broth. You can vary it by adding herbs, substituting other vegetables for those listed, or by using chicken parts instead of a whole chicken. Not only will you have wonderful homemade broth on hand but also a quantity of cooked chicken you can use in a number of recipes, such as homemade chicken noodle soup, chicken salad, pizza, sandwiches, pasta, and casseroles.

2 large carrots, scrubbed and cut into chunks

1 (3- to 3½-pound) whole chicken or bone-in chicken parts

2 large stalks of celery with leaves, cut into chunks

1 large onion, quartered

5 sprigs of parsley

Salt and pepper to taste

5 to 6 cups water

YIELD: 6 to 8 cups
SLOW COOKER SIZE: 4 or 6 quart
PREP TIME: 10 minutes
COOKING TIME: 8 to 10 hours on LOW

1. Place all ingredients in slow cooker in order listed, with enough water to fill the pot about three-quarters full. (Use 6-quart slow cooker for whole chicken.)

2. Cover and cook on LOW heat for 6 hours.

3. Remove chicken from pot, cut the meat from the bones, and save for other uses.

4. Return stripped bones to pot and continue cooking for 2 to 4 more hours.

5. If not using immediately, allow the broth to cool about 1 hour and then strain it. Line a colander with cheesecloth and place it in a

Serving Suggestions

This broth is a wonderful base for homemade chicken noodle soup. If you store it in small containers in the freezer, it will come in very handy in any recipe calling for chicken broth. We couldn't make risotto without it!

Variations

You can add dried herbs, such as thyme, marjoram, or a few bay leaves or fresh herbs 15 minutes before the stock is done.

Vary the vegetables to suit your own personal preferences, but avoid very strong vegetables, such as broccoli or cabbage.

large bowl. Pour the contents of the pot into the colander. Discard the carcass and vegetables.

6. Refrigerate the broth for up to 3 days or store in 1- to 2-cup containers in the freezer for several months.

Tip

When pouring the heated contents of a slow cooker pot into a bowl, we suggest placing the bowl in the sink and pouring the contents of the slow cooker into it there. If you accidently spill, cleanup will be easy.

*B*asic Beef or Veal Stock

Make this once a month, store in small containers in the freezer, and you'll never have to resort to bouillon cubes again! We had to use the large 6-quart slow cooker for this recipe to accommodate all the bones, but you could cut the recipe in half to use the 4-quart cooker. What to do with the cooked bones? If you're a dog owner, Fido will jump for joy if you toss one his way. You could also use the meat from the bones in a roast beef hash or stir-fry meal.

4 pounds meaty beef and/or veal bones

2 large onions, peeled and quartered

2 large carrots, scrubbed and cut into large chunks

4 cloves garlic, peeled

2 large stalks of celery with leaves, cut into large chunks

6 sprigs fresh parsley

1 tablespoon dried thyme

2 bay leaves

1 teaspoon salt

1 teaspoon freshly ground black pepper

8 cups water

1. Preheat oven to 450°F.

2. Place bones, onions, carrots, and garlic on rimmed baking sheet and roast in the oven, turning bones after 10 minutes, for 25 to 30 minutes, until bones and vegetables are browned.

3. Place all ingredients in slow cooker and add enough water to fill about ¾ full. Stir to combine. Cover and cook on LOW for 10 to 12 hours. Allow to cool to room temperature.

YIELD: about 2 quarts

SLOW COOKER SIZE: 6 quart

PREP TIME: 15 minutes

COOKING TIME: 10 to 12 hours on LOW

Serving Suggestions

Use this in homemade vegetable or French onion soup, risotto, beef stew, gravies and sauces.

Variations

You can substitute leeks for the onions and various other herbs. Avoid substituting any strong-flavored vegetables, such as cabbage or broccoli, which would overwhelm the delicate beef flavor of the broth.

Tip

This recipe is also a good way to use up leftover bones from roasts, preferably with a little meat still left on them. Toss them in a freezer bag, label, and use once you've collected enough for a good broth. Thaw them before using.

4. Strain through a fine sieve or a colander lined with cheesecloth into a large bowl. Cover and refrigerate. Once chilled, you can remove fat from the surface of the stock. Use within 3 days or freeze in small containers up to 3 months.

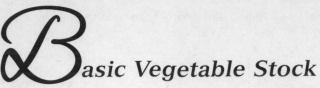asic Vegetable Stock

Vary the vegetables or herbs and you can change the flavor of this broth in countless ways. It's the perfect stock for risotto or homemade soups if you're a vegetarian. You'll want to make and freeze portions of this stock on a regular basis. Freeze in small 1-pint containers or ice cube trays.

4 large carrots, scrubbed and cut into chunks

2 parsnips, scrubbed and cut into chunks

6 stalks of celery with leaves, washed and cut into chunks

3 medium potatoes, scrubbed and quartered

1 large onion, peeled and quartered

3 cloves garlic, chopped

6 sprigs of parsley

1 teaspoon dried thyme

½ teaspoon dried oregano

1 bay leaf

Salt and pepper to taste

8 cups water

1. Place all ingredients in slow cooker.

2. Cover and cook on LOW heat for 4 to 5 hours.

3. If not using immediately, allow the stock to cool about 1 hour and then strain it. Place a colander in a large bowl and pour the contents of the pot into it. Discard the vegetables. Refrigerate the broth for up to 3 days, or store in 1- to 2-cup containers in the freezer for several months.

YIELD: about 1½ quarts	
SLOW COOKER SIZE: 4 quart	
PREP TIME: 15 minutes	
COOKING TIME: 4 to 5 hours on LOW	

Serving Suggestions

This stock is a wonderful base for homemade vegetarian soups. If you store it in small containers in the freezer, it will come in very handy in any recipe calling for broth.

Variations

You can add cayenne pepper or crushed red pepper flakes to heat it up.

Vary the vegetables to suit your own personal preferences, but any very strong-flavored one, such as broccoli, cauliflower, or cabbage, will overpower other flavors and may not marry well with ingredients in other recipes to which you add it.

Start a veggie bag in the freezer, so that during the week when you have leftover parsley, celery, or a few extra carrots on hand, you can bank them for your next batch of vegetable stock.

*M*onday's Vegetable Soup

This easy-to-make, basic vegetable soup is a boon to the weight watcher. It's low in calories and chock full of things that are good for you. Make a big pot of it every Monday and you'll start the week off right, with enough left over for a quick, healthy lunch or dinner later in the week. (Note: this recipe uses the large 6-quart slow cooker.)

1 cup peeled and sliced carrots

1 cup peeled and chopped onions

1 cup sliced celery

2 cloves garlic, minced

8 cups water

4 teaspoons concentrated beef or vegetable base, such as Better than Bouillon*

2 (16-ounce) cans diced tomatoes, undrained

2 cups diced cabbage

1 pound frozen or canned green beans, drained, or 2 cups fresh green beans, trimmed

1 cup frozen peas

1 cup frozen corn

1 cup diced zucchini

2 teaspoons Italian seasoning

1 pinch crushed red pepper flakes

Salt and pepper to taste

½ cup brown rice

1. Place all ingredients except rice in slow cooker. Cover and cook on LOW heat for 6 to 8 hours.

2. Add rice, cover and cook 1 more hour on HIGH.

SERVES: 6

SLOW COOKER SIZE: 6 quart

PREP TIME: 15 minutes

COOKING TIME: 6 to 8 hours on LOW, 1 hour on HIGH

Serving Suggestions

Serve with whole wheat rolls and treat yourself to a little nonfat frozen yogurt for dessert.

Freeze any leftovers in 2-cup containers for quick, healthy meals another day.

Variations

To use a 4-quart slow cooker, cut this recipe in half.

For a heartier soup, add 1 pound browned hamburger or beef stew meat.

Add 2 cups peeled and diced potatoes at the start instead of the rice.

Add 1 cup uncooked whole wheat macaroni, instead of the rice, and cook 1 hour on HIGH.

Add 1 cup diced squash.

Add ½ green pepper, chopped.

Add 1 can kidney beans, drained and rinsed.

You can substitute 8 cups homemade stock for the soup base and water.

Tip

*If you can't find the Better than Bouillon beef or vegetable soup bases in your grocery store, you can substitute 4 bouillon cubes.

$\mathcal{S}$imple Pasta Sauce

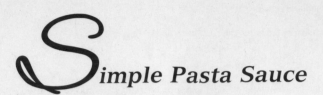

Once you make our simple pasta sauce, you'll never have to buy bottled pasta sauce again! We think you'll find this sauce and its variations so easy to prepare and so good, that you'll make it on a regular basis. This easy sauce is even better cooked the night before and then rewarmed the next day before serving. You can use it on chicken cacciatore, chicken parmigiana, meat loaf, pizza, and over sausage and peppers.

¹/₄ cup olive oil

1 large onion, peeled and chopped

1 medium carrot, peeled and finely chopped or grated

1 stalk celery, finely chopped

3 cloves garlic, peeled and minced

2 (28-ounce) cans crushed tomatoes in puree

¹/₂ cup dry red wine (optional)

¹/₈ to ¹/₄ teaspoon red pepper flakes to taste

1 tablespoon dried parsley flakes

1 teaspoon dried oregano

1 teaspoon dried basil

1 teaspoon sugar

Salt and pepper to taste

1. In a medium nonstick skillet over medium heat, sauté the onion, carrot, and celery in the olive oil until the onions are soft, about 3 minutes. Add the garlic and sauté 1 minute more. Pour into the slow cooker.

2. Add the rest of the ingredients and stir to combine. Cover and cook on LOW for 8 to 10 hours, stirring once or twice if you're home

YIELD: about 6 cups, enough to sauce 2 pounds of pasta

SLOW COOKER SIZE: 4 quart

PREP TIME: 15 minutes

COOKING TIME: 8 to 10 hours on LOW

Serving Suggestions

This sauce is good poured over freshly cooked pasta or reduced down about 30 minutes and used as a pizza sauce.

Variations

Substitute 2 (14-ounce) cans Italian seasoned diced tomatoes, crushed with an immersion blender, for one 28-ounce can crushed tomatoes.

You can add ground beef, meatballs, or Italian sausage by browning first then adding to the pot. Mushrooms and chopped bell peppers can also be added.

If you prefer fresh herbs, substitute 1 tablespoon

while it cooks. If desired, you can thicken the sauce slightly by turning the heat to HIGH and removing the lid during the last hour of cooking.

3. Taste before serving. If necessary, reseason with a dash of salt, pepper, and any other flavors that may have cooked out. For a chunky sauce, serve as is. For a smoother sauce, blend slightly with an immersion blender.

oregano, 1 tablespoon basil, and 3 tablespoons parsley for the dried herbs and add them to your sauce during the last hour of cooking.

To cut the preparation time in half, use packaged items, such as shredded carrots, frozen chopped onions, bottled chopped garlic, and substitute 2 teaspoons Italian seasoning for the oregano and basil.

Tip

If you can find them, use premium crushed tomatoes, such as San Marzano or Muir Glen brands.

Do not used bottled wines that are labeled "cooking wine." Never cook with a wine that you wouldn't want to drink.

$\mathcal{L}$ois's Pizza Sauce

If you make pizza weekly, as we do, it's great to have one-cup containers of this wonderful sauce on hand in the freezer. Lois likes some texture to her pizza sauce, but if you prefer a smoother sauce, you can puree it with an immersion blender when done.

¼ cup olive oil

3 medium onions, peeled and chopped

9 cloves garlic, minced

6 tablespoons tomato paste

3 (28-ounce) cans crushed tomatoes in puree

3 tablespoons sugar

2 tablespoons dried Italian seasoning

2 teaspoons salt

½ to 1 teaspoon dried red pepper flakes or to taste

1. In a large skillet, heat the oil over medium heat. Add the onion and sauté until soft, about 3 minutes. Add the garlic and cook 1 more minute. Remove from heat and transfer to the slow cooker.

2. Place remaining ingredients in slow cooker and stir to combine. Cover and cook on LOW for 5 hours. Remove lid, increase heat to HIGH and cook 3 more hours, stirring occasionally.

3. Taste before serving. If necessary, reseason with a dash of salt and any other flavors that may have cooked out. Also, if you prefer a smoother sauce, puree with an immersion blender.

YIELD: about 3 quarts

SLOW COOKER SIZE: 4 quart

PREP TIME: 25 minutes

COOKING TIME: 5 hours on LOW and 3 hours on HIGH

Serving Suggestions

If you have a bread machine, here's a simple pizza dough from our book *More Bread Machine Magic* that you can make in minutes:

1 cup water
2 tablespoons olive oil
1 tablespoon sugar
1 teaspoon salt
3 cups flour
2 teaspoons yeast

This dough will keep in an oiled plastic bag in the refrigerator up to 3 days until needed.

Variations

You can substitute ¼ cup chopped fresh basil and 2 tablespoons fresh oregano for the dried Italian seasoning. Stir in during the last half hour of cooking.

4. Use about 1 cup of this sauce to top a 12- to 14-inch pizza. Store the leftovers in 1-cup containers in the freezer for future use.

Tip

If you prefer crispy pizza crusts, use a pizza stone or one of those pizza pans that has lots of small holes in it to allow the hot air to reach the bottom of the crust.

$\mathcal{O}$ld Faithful Pot Roast

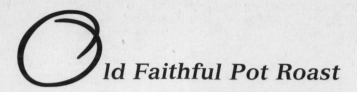

Before slow cookers came on the scene, this is the roast we all used to make if gravy making wasn't our forte. It was quick to throw together, and best of all made its own gravy. Wrapped in foil and baked several hours in the oven, this roast was always a sure hit at the Sunday night dinner table. The recipe survives and is a natural for the slow cooker. It's an oldie but a goodie—not only delicious but high in comfort-food value.

2 cans cream of mushroom soup

1 (1-ounce) package of dry onion soup mix

2½ to 3½ pounds rump, chuck, or tri-tip pot roast, well trimmed

Salt and pepper, if desired

SERVES: 6
SLOW COOKER SIZE: 4½ quart
PREP TIME: 10 minutes
COOKING TIME: 6 to 8 hours on LOW

1. In slow cooker, stir the soups together. Place the pot roast in the pot and coat well with the soup mixture.

2. Cover and cook on LOW heat for 6 to 8 hours.

3. Season with salt and pepper, if desired, before serving.

Serving Suggestions

Keeping with the comfort food theme, this is great served with creamy mashed potatoes and steamed green peas. For something different, try slicing very thin and serving over cooked fettucine noodles like a stroganoff, with boiled pearl onions on the side.

Variations

For a more flavorful roast, brown it first. Warm 1 to 2 tablespoons oil in a large Dutch oven over medium-high heat on the stove, add the roast and brown all sides. Transfer the roast and its juices to the slow cooker.

You could add several cloves of garlic, Worcestershire sauce, sliced onion, or sliced fresh mushrooms.

This recipe also works beautifully with 3 pounds frozen meatballs, thawed. Add 1 cup of water. Serve over mashed potatoes, noodles, or rice.

Tip

If your pot roast is a little too long for your slow cooker pot, just cut it in half and arrange each half to fit inside the pot side by side.

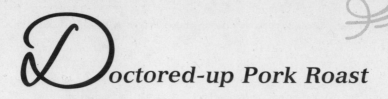

Doctored-up Pork Roast

The inspiration for this simple roast came from Lois's friend Judy Self, whose neighbor shared it with her. She likes to cook pork roasts in Coke and packaged onion soup mix. We substituted Dr. Pepper and were very pleased with the results. This could easily become a weekly standard. And you could work wonders with the tasty leftovers in just minutes.

4 pound pork loin, shoulder, or Boston butt pork roast, trimmed of fat.

1 (12-ounce) can or bottle Dr. Pepper

1 (1-ounce) package dry onion soup mix

Salt and pepper, if desired

FOR GRAVY (OPTIONAL)

½ cup flour

½ cup water

1. Place roast in slow cooker and pour soda and soup mix on top. Cover and cook on LOW for 8 to 10 hours.

2. Remove roast and let sit for about 10 minutes before slicing.

3. You can also make a quick gravy by carefully pouring the juices from the slow cooker into a deep skillet on the stove. With a large spoon, skim as much fat as possible off the top of the juices, then bring remaining liquid to a boil over medium-high heat. Reduce heat to a gentle boil.

SERVES: 6

SLOW COOKER SIZE: 4 quart

PREP TIME: 5 minutes

COOKING TIME: 8 to 10 hours on LOW

Serving Suggestions

Serve this with the Veggie Mash (page 232) or regular mashed potatoes and lima beans. Leftover meat can be shredded and combined with barbeque sauce for quick and easy BBQ pork sandwiches on warmed hamburger buns or used in our "Fried Rice" recipe (see page 76), or wrapped in tortillas as burritos or added to hearty soups.

Variations

You could substitute other sodas, such as cola, orange, or even root beer!

4. In a small bowl, whisk together flour and water. Gradually pour into the juices in the skillet, whisking well to avoid lumps. Cook until the gravy thickens. Season to taste with salt and pepper, if desired.

Tip

If you can't find the soda in 12-ounce cans, just measure out 1½ cups from a large bottle.

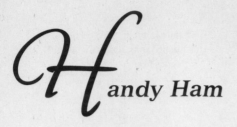andy Ham

Here's a basic ham recipe, one you can rely on for a quick and easy dinner. Even better, you can easily double the recipe, then use the leftovers for other quick meals, such as our Ham, Sweet Potatoes, and Onions recipe (see page 62); Ham and Eggs with O'Brien Potatoes (see page 39); ham salad sandwiches; ham loaf; in navy bean or split pea soup; green beans and ham; or even combined with pineapple atop a pizza.

¼ cup orange marmalade

1½ teaspoons Dijon mustard

1 3-pound, fully cooked, boneless ham

1. In a small bowl, combine the marmalade and mustard

2. Place the ham in the slow cooker and spoon the marmalade mixture on top.

3. Cover and cook on LOW for 6 to 8 hours. Allow to stand for 5 to 10 minutes before slicing.

SERVES: 6

SLOW COOKER SIZE: 4 quart

PREP TIME: 5 minutes

COOKING TIME: 6 to 8 hours on LOW

Serving Suggestions

Serve with au gratin potatoes and steamed green peas and pearl onions.

Little Hershey's Kisses scattered on the dinner table would be a festive touch and a simple dessert.

Variations

You can substitute apricot preserves or peach preserves for the marmalade and a horseradish mustard for the Dijon. (You can make your own horseradish mustard by adding a tiny pinch of prepared horseradish to the 1½ teaspoons Dijon mustard.)

Tip

Since the ham is fully cooked to begin with, you can cook it in half the time if you're in a hurry. It just needs to be heated through.

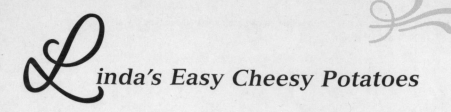

Linda's Easy Cheesy Potatoes

We encourage you to try the recipe as written or expand on it to your heart's delight—its just a starting point. See our list of variations for several ideas. We think you'll find this easy side dish a star in your repertoire.

1 pint sour cream

1 (10-ounce) can cream of potato soup

1 (30-ounce) package Ore-Ida shredded hash brown
   potatoes

1 large onion, peeled and chopped

2 cups (8 ounces) shredded cheddar cheese

Salt and pepper to taste

Place all ingredients in slow cooker and stir to combine. Cover and cook on LOW for 5 to 7 hours.

SERVES: 5

SLOW COOKER SIZE: 4 quart

PREP TIME: 15 minutes

COOKING TIME: 5 to 7 hours on LOW

Serving Suggestions

For an easy dinner, serve with grilled ham steak and steamed carrots. A cobbler for dessert would be peachy!

Variations

To lighten up, substitute either reduced-fat sour cream or a second can of potato soup for the regular sour cream. You could also omit the cheese or cut the amount in half.

To vary this recipe, try adding things such as diced green chiles, diced green pepper, chives, cooked and crumbled bacon, diced ham, garlic, dill, or Italian seasoning. For a switch, vary the types of soup. You could also vary the potatoes and use frozen O'Brien potatoes instead. And if you're having problems getting children to eat their vegetables or using up leftover vegetables, add the veggies to this casserole and watch them disappear!

Tip

When cutting vegetables, especially round ones like onions, it's best to cut them in half first so you'll have a flat surface when you start slicing them.

*B*asic Risotto

This is another recipe that you can alter at will. We love to include things like shrimp, asparagus, tomatoes, mushrooms, roasted sweet potatoes, caramelized onions, lemon zest, roasted garlic, various herbs—the list goes on and on.

3 tablespoons butter

1 onion, finely peeled and chopped

1½ cups arborio rice

½ cup dry white wine

2 (14-ounce) cans chicken broth

¼ teaspoon salt

½ teaspoon pepper

½ cup warm water

Juice of ½ lemon

½ cup grated Parmesan cheese

SERVES: 6
SLOW COOKER SIZE: 4 quart
PREP TIME: 10 minutes
COOKING TIME: 2½ to 3 hours on HIGH

1. In a nonstick skillet over medium heat, sauté the onion in the butter until soft, about 4 minutes. Pour into slow cooker.

2. Stir in the remaining ingredients, except for the water, lemon juice, and Parmesan cheese. Cover and cook on HIGH for 2½ to 3 hours, until all the liquid is absorbed by the rice. Stir in the warm water, lemon juice, and Parmesan cheese. Cover and cook about 5 minutes longer until heated through.

Serving Suggestions

For a scrumptious meal, combine this with grilled seafood, such as scallops or shrimp, and grilled or oven-roasted asparagus. (Marinate asparagus in a balsamic vinaigrette dressing. Place on hot grill or large baking sheet in a single layer. Grill or roast in 425°F oven for about 10 minutes. Sprinkle with toasted, sliced almonds and serve.)

Variations

If you like your risotto very creamy, stir in 1 to 2 more tablespoons butter very gently with a wooden spoon just before adding the Parmesan cheese.

You can use this as a side dish or stir in seafood and a vegetable to convert it into the main course.

Tip

Leftover risotto does not reheat well. Best to first warm it in the microwave a little, then stir in hot liquid.

$\mathcal{B}$read Pudding Galore

This is a basic recipe to which you can add all kinds of extras or vary the type of bread to create hundreds of new bread puddings! If you're a prolific baker who always has leftover bread on hand, this is the recipe for you!

1 pound firm-textured white bread, such as French or Italian, cut into 1-inch cubes (about 12 cups)

½ cup melted butter

2 cups whole milk

4 eggs

¾ cup dark brown sugar

½ teaspoon salt

1 teaspoon ground cinnamon

¼ teaspoon ground nutmeg

¼ teaspoon ground cloves

1 cup chopped dried fruit or 2 cups chopped fresh fruit, optional

OPTIONAL SAUCE:

1 pint good quality vanilla ice cream, melted

SERVES: 4 to 5
SLOW COOKER SIZE: 4 quart
PREP TIME: 10 minutes
COOKING TIME: 2 hours on HIGH then 2 to 3 hours on LOW

Variations

To lighten up, reduce the butter to 5 tablespoons and substitute 1% milk for the whole milk. Use 2 eggs and ½ cup Egg Beaters. Use ½ cup brown sugar and omit the optional sauce.

You can add one or more of the following to this recipe: dried fruit, fresh apples or pears, chopped nuts, or frozen berries

Vary the bread: use brioche, challah, whole wheat raisin, oatmeal, cracked wheat, etc.

Tip

Melt the ice cream by placing it in the refrigerator overnight. Pour into a small pitcher for serving.

1. In the slow cooker, toss bread cubes with melted butter.

2. In a large bowl, whisk together the milk, eggs, sugar, salt, and spices. Pour over bread, sprinkle with fruit if desired, and gently stir until all the bread is coated with the mixture.

3. Cover and cook on HIGH for 2 hours. Reduce heat to LOW, gently stir, cover, and cook 2 to 3 hours more.

4. Serve warm with vanilla ice cream "sauce" on top, if desired.

Spring

Spring

Hot Pickled Carrots

Franks A Lot!

Sticky Wings

Chili Con Queso Dip

Ham and Eggs with O'Brien
Potatoes

Cinco de Mayo Eggs

Spicy Tortilla Soup

Pozole

Zuppa Romana

Missy's Easy Meatball Minestrone

Tomato Cream Sauce with Vodka

Frijoles Refritos (Refried Beans)

Homemade Pastrami

Lentil Chili

Lite Turkey Chili

Rosemary Lamb Stew

Down-Home Beef Stew

New England Boiled Dinner

Ham, Sweet Potatoes, and Onions

Marsha's Pork Chops, Potatoes,
and Sauerkraut

Carnitas

Poulet Provençal

Braised Lamb Shanks

Ginger's Five-Spice Chicken

Turkey Breast with Ginger-Orange
Glaze

Enchilada Stack

Risotto Primavera

Slow Cooker "Fried" Rice

Deep-Dish Dinner

Southern-Style Green Beans

Savory Mashed Potatoes

Celia's Freezable Applesauce

Pineapple Upside-down Carrot
Cake

Butterscotch Pudding Cake

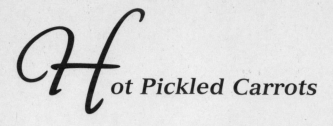ot Pickled Carrots

Some like it hot; some like it hotter. If you want to kick up the temperature on these, just substitute a hotter pepper such as the serrano, habanero, or Scotch bonnet. These make a good healthy snack or side dish.

8 cups sliced carrots (approximately 14 large),
   peeled and diagonally sliced ¼-inch thick
1 (7-ounce) can or jar of whole jalapeño peppers,
   undrained
1 onion, sliced
1 tablespoon vegetable oil
½ cup white wine vinegar

Place all ingredients in slow cooker and stir to combine. Cover and cook on LOW for 4 hours or on HIGH for 2 hours. The carrots should be cooked but still slightly crunchy. Remove from slow cooker and place in clean jars and store in the refrigerator. Chill at least 4 hours before serving.

SERVES: 12
SLOW COOKER SIZE: 4 quart
PREP TIME: 15 minutes
COOKING TIME: 4 hours on LOW or 2 hours on HIGH

Serving Suggestions

They can be served as a side dish with a Mexican meal or layered in a sandwich.

Variations

Don't know what to do with the leftovers? Try chopping up about ½ cup and tossing them in a meat loaf mixture. Wonderful!

Tip

When handling hot peppers, keep hands away from your eyes and always wear rubber gloves.

$\mathcal{F}$ranks A Lot!

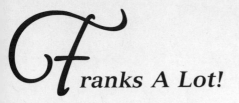

Have you ever been to a party where the meatballs or cocktail franks weren't the first appetizer to disappear? Your guests will thank you if you double this recipe and bring out a second batch when the first one vanishes.

1 (8-ounce) can tomato sauce

2 tablespoons water

2 tablespoons red wine vinegar

1 (1.5-ounce) envelope dry spaghetti sauce mix

1 tablespoon sugar

$^1/_4$ teaspoon dry mustard

2 pounds cocktail franks, smokie links, or kosher
   hot dogs, cut into 1-inch pieces

Place all ingredients in slow cooker and stir to combine. Cover and cook on HIGH for 2 hours. These can be served from the slow cooker and will keep for hours on the WARM or LOW setting.

SERVES: 12	
SLOW COOKER SIZE: 4 quart	
PREP TIME: 10 minutes	
COOKING TIME: 2 hours on HIGH	

Serving Suggestions

Have plenty of toothpicks placed next to the pot and a trash can nearby for disposal.

Variations

To really speed up preparation, substitute 1¼ cups of your favorite spaghetti sauce for the first 6 ingredients.

Tip

Kosher hot dogs hold up better over time than regular hot dogs, which tend to get rather mushy.

Sticky Wings

This is the perfect appetizer for a gathering of football fans. See our variations for ways to turn these into Buffalo wings, BBQ wings, or teriyaki wings.

2 dozen chicken wings

1 (6-ounce) can frozen orange juice concentrate, thawed

½ cup honey

2 teaspoons freshly grated ginger

2 teaspoons salt

½ to 1 teaspoon cayenne pepper to taste

1. Cut chicken wings in half at the joint and remove the tips. Place chicken wings under broiler, about 4 to 6 inches from the heat. Broil about 15 to 20 minutes until brown, turning once after 10 minutes.

2. Meanwhile, place the remaining ingredients in the slow cooker and stir to combine.

3. Add the wings to the slow cooker and gently stir to coat them with the sauce. Cover and cook on LOW for 2 to 3 hours, until hot.

4. Taste before serving. If necessary, reseason with a dash of salt, pepper, and any other flavors that may have cooked out.

SERVES: 12

SLOW COOKER SIZE: 4 quart

PREP TIME: 15 minutes

COOKING TIME: 2 to 3 hours on LOW

Serving Suggestions

Serve these as an hors d'oeuvre with plenty of paper napkins nearby.

Variations

Turn these into Buffalo wings by substituting ¼ cup hot sauce and ½ cup melted butter for the sauce.

Turn these into barbeque wings by substituting 2 cups of barbeque sauce for the sauce.

Turn these into teriyaki wings by substituting 1 cup soy sauce, 1 cup brown sugar, ¼ cup Japanese rice wine or sherry, and 2 teaspoons freshly grated ginger for the sauce. Or even easier, substitute 2 cups bottled teriyaki sauce rather than making your own.

Don't discard the wing tips. Toss them into a bag, freeze, and then add them to the pot next time you make chicken stock.

Chili Con Queso Dip

Here's an old standby that's always a hit with a crowd.

2 (15-ounce) cans chili con carne without beans
2 (8-ounce) packages cream cheese, softened
Tortilla chips or corn chips, for dipping

1. Place chili and cream cheese in slow cooker. Cover and cook on HIGH for 2 hours, stirring once after 1 hour to blend in the melting cream cheese.

2. Reduce heat to LOW or WARM and serve right out of the slow cooker with tortilla chips or corn chips for dipping.

SERVES: 10

SLOW COOKER SIZE:
1½ quart

PREP TIME: 5 minutes

COOKING TIME: 2 hours on HIGH

Serving Suggestions

You could also serve this inside a hollowed out round loaf of bread and reheat in the microwave when necessary.

Variations

To lighten up this dip, use reduced fat or fat-free cream cheese.

Tip

To quickly soften cream cheese, remove it from the foil wrapper, place on a plate and microwave on HIGH about 45 seconds.

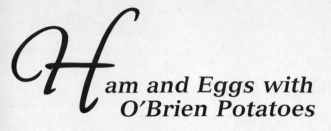am and Eggs with O'Brien Potatoes

This is an entire brunch for six in one pot. How easy is that?

2 tablespoons vegetable oil

1 (24-ounce) package frozen O'Brien potatoes (frozen potatoes with chopped onions and green peppers)

1 ham steak (about 1 pound), cut into small cubes

12 eggs

³/₄ cup evaporated milk

Salt and pepper to taste

Chopped fresh parsley to garnish

1. Heat the oil in a large nonstick skillet over medium-high heat. Add the potatoes and the diced ham; cook as directed on the package until golden brown. Place in the slow cooker.

2. In a large bowl, whisk together the eggs, milk, and salt and pepper to taste. Pour over the potatoes and stir to combine.

3. Cover and cook on LOW for 3 to 4 hours. Serve with a sprinkle of parsley on top to garnish.

SERVES: 6	
SLOW COOKER SIZE: 4 quart	
PREP TIME: 15 minutes	
COOKING TIME: 3 to 4 hours on LOW	

 Serving Suggestions

Serve with a cold glass of V-8 or tomato juice and a large fruit salad to complete the meal.

Variations

You could sprinkle a little shredded cheddar cheese on top before serving.

To lighten, find the fat-free O'Brien potatoes in the freezer section of your market, substitute 1 pound turkey ham or turkey bacon for the ham steak, substitute 2 cups Egg Beaters for 8 of the whole eggs, and use evaporated skim milk.

Tip

If you're concerned about calories, evaporated milk also comes in fat-free and low-fat varieties.

Cinco de Mayo Eggs

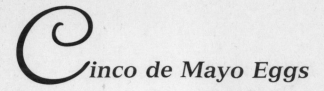

These festive breakfast burritos are perfect for a brunch potluck or buffet. You can set the pot right on the buffet table, surrounded with the garnishes, and let people help themselves.

1 pound chorizo, casing removed (see Tip)

1 onion, finely chopped

1 (7-ounce) can diced green chiles or jalapeño peppers

18 eggs

1 cup evaporated milk

1 teaspoon salt

¼ teaspoon pepper

12 warm 8-inch flour tortillas

OPTIONAL GARNISHES:

salsa, or chopped tomatoes and cilantro

shredded cheddar and/or Monterey jack cheese

sour cream

sliced black or green olives

guacamole or diced avocado

1. In a large skillet over medium heat, cook the chorizo and onion about 7 minutes until the onions are soft and the chorizo is crumbled. Pour into a colander and drain well.

2. While the chorizo and onion cook, in the slow cooker whisk together the eggs, milk, salt and pepper. Stir in the chorizo mixture and chiles, cover, and cook on LOW 4 to 5 hours.

3. Serve directly from the slow cooker. Place two or three spoonfuls on a warm flour tortilla with garnishes of choice and roll up.

SERVES: 8	
SLOW COOKER SIZE: 4 quart	
PREP TIME: 15 minutes	
COOKING TIME: 4 to 5 hours on LOW	

Serving Suggestions

If you have a colorful Mexican blanket, it makes a perfect tablecloth for a meal like this. Add a plate of orange slices or a fresh fruit salad, a basket of warm tortillas wrapped in a colorful cloth napkin, and small bowls of the various garnishes. Then your guests can create their own burritos.

Variations

Chorizo is a spicy Mexican sausage. You could easily substitute linguisa, Italian sausage, or even just plain pork sausage, casings removed.

Tip

Chorizo sausages vary greatly from one brand to another. If you purchased the solid sausage variety, you'll need to chop up the chorizo before adding it to the skillet.

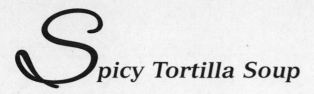picy Tortilla Soup

This soup would be a wonderful starter for any Mexican or Spanish meal. It's a fiesta in a bowl!

4 (10-ounce) cans condensed onion soup, undiluted

2 cups water

2 (10-ounce) or 4 (6-ounce) cans Snap-E-Tom
   tomato cocktail or spicy V-8 juice or any spicy
   vegetable juice

1 (16-ounce) bottle salsa verde (green chili sauce)

1 teaspoon ground coriander or cumin

About 8 ounces tortilla chips, broken into bite-size
   pieces

2 cups (8 ounces) Monterey jack cheese, grated

1. Place all ingredients in slow cooker, except tortilla chips and cheese. Stir to combine. Cover and cook on LOW for 6 to 8 hours.

2. Place a small handful of tortilla chips in the bottom of each soup bowl. Ladle the soup into the bowls and top each with some cheese.

3. Taste before serving. If necessary, reseason with a dash of salt, pepper, and any other flavors that may have cooked out.

SERVES: 8
SLOW COOKER SIZE: 4½ quart
PREP TIME: 10 minutes
COOKING TIME: 6 to 8 hours on LOW

Serving Suggestions

It's fun to serve this as a first course to go with a "build-your-own taco bar" for your family or friends. If you have a large kitchen and enough family members, everyone can be responsible for preparing one or two items to go on the taco bar. Or ask guests to bring specific items. End the meal with a small bowl of vanilla ice cream drizzled with butterscotch sauce and chopped nuts.

Variations

For a slightly different flavor, try cheddar cheese as a topping and sprinkle with cilantro. You can also use chipotle chili sauce in place of the salsa verde.

Tip

To save time, purchase packaged grated cheese for this soup.

Pozole

This simple Mexican soup is all about the garnishes, making it a fun dish to serve to a crowd. Cook up a pot of the soup and set out bowls of various garnishes that guests can add as strikes their fancy. It's perfect with a margarita.

2 tablespoons vegetable oil

2½ pounds boneless pork butt, shoulder, or loin roast, trimmed of fat and cut into a few large chunks, or 2½ pounds boneless country-style ribs, trimmed of fat and cut into a few large chunks

4 cloves garlic, peeled and chopped

½ white onion, peeled and chopped

1 tablespoon kosher salt

Pepper to taste

2 teaspoons ground cumin

½ teaspoon dried oregano

¾ ounce (about 3 large pods) dried ancho or New Mexico chiles, cut in half and stems and seeds removed

4 cups water

4 cups chicken broth (preferably homemade)

1 (28-ounce) can hominy, drained and rinsed

OPTIONAL ACCOMPANIMENTS:

chopped lettuce

diced avocado

thinly sliced cabbage

chopped white onion

sliced radishes

lime wedges

fried thin strips of corn tortillas

SERVES: 6

SLOW COOKER SIZE: 4 quart

PREP TIME: 25 minutes

COOKING TIME: 8 to 10 hours on LOW

Serving Suggestions

Serve this with a grapefruit, avocado, red onion salad. Arrange alternate slices of 2 avocados and the sections of 2 grapefruits on a serving plate. Whisk together 1 teaspoon grapefruit juice, 2 teaspoons red wine vinegar, 3 tablespoons olive oil, and salt and pepper to taste. Drizzle over the salad and scatter a handful of finely chopped red onion on top.

Add a plate of homemade cornbread, and a decadent dessert, like a warm, fudgy brownie topped with a dollop of ice cream and chocolate sauce.

Variations

To lighten up, replace the pork with an equal amount of boneless chicken thighs after 4 hours or firm fish fillets added the last hour.

fried pork rinds

dried red pepper flakes

dried oregano leaves

shredded Monterey jack cheese

fresh chopped cilantro

sour cream

minced fresh jalapeño peppers

Tip

If you don't have an immersion blender and need to puree this in a blender, do so with care. Ladle the hot soup into the blender in small batches to avoid erruptions of hot soup when you turn it on.

To serve diced avocado as a garnish, cut it up at the last minute and drizzle with some lemon juice to prevent it from turning brown immediately. All other garnishes can be assembled in advance, covered, and set aside.

1. In a large skillet, heat oil over medium-high heat. Add pork and brown all sides well, about 10 minutes. Drain off fat.

2. Place all ingredients except the hominy and accompaniments in the slow cooker. Stir to combine.

3. Cover and cook on LOW for 8 to 10 hours until the pork is tender.

4. Remove pork from slow cooker and shred with two forks.

5. With an immersion blender, puree the remaining ingredients in the slow cooker. (For a slightly milder flavor, you can remove the chili pods first.)

6. Return the pork to the pot, along with the hominy. Heat through and serve with small bowls of selected accompaniments.

$\mathcal{Z}$uppa Romana

This hearty main course soup is a family pleaser. It's also a good soup for using up leftover grilled sausages. Cut them up and toss them into the pot and you can skip the first step.

1 tablespoon olive oil

³/₄ pound hot Italian sausage, sliced ¹/₂-inch thick

³/₄ pound smoked sausage, such as kielbasa, sliced
   ¹/₂-inch thick

2 large onions, chopped

1 clove garlic, minced

2 tablespoon chopped fresh parsley

1 cup dry red wine, such as a cabernet or chianti

1 medium zucchini, diced into ¹/₂-inch pieces

1 medium green pepper, stemmed, seeded, and
   diced into ¹/₂-inch pieces

1 (28-ounce) can crushed tomatoes in puree

1 (10¹/₂-ounce) can condensed beef broth

1 soup can–ful water

1 teaspoon dried basil

1 teaspoon dried oregano

Salt and pepper, to taste

4 ounces orzo or bowtie pasta

Parmesan cheese garnish

1. In a large nonstick skillet, heat the oil over medium heat. Add the sausages and cook until browned, about 8 minutes. Transfer to the slow cooker with a slotted spoon.

2. Add the onion to the same skillet and cook until softened, about 3 minutes. Add the garlic and parsley; cook 1 minute more. Stir in

SERVES: 4

SLOW COOKER SIZE: 4 quart

PREP TIME: 30 minutes

COOKING TIME: 6 to 8 hours on LOW

Serving Suggestions

Serve it with warm foccacia bread and ice cream sandwiches for dessert.

Variations

You can substitute 1 more cup of beef broth for the wine, if desired.

To make this soup even heartier, substitute 8 ounces cheese tortellini for the pasta.

You could also substitute 1 can drained cannellini beans for the pasta.

To lighten up the recipe, substitute turkey sausages for the Italian and smoked sausages.

Tip

Treat fresh herbs as you would freshly picked flowers. Cut a little off the stems and place

the wine, bring to a boil, and scrape up any browned bits off the bottom of the pan. Pour the mixture into the slow cooker

3. Add the zucchini, green pepper, tomatoes, broth, and water, basil, oregano, salt and pepper, to the slow cooker and stir to combine. Cover and cook on LOW for 6 to 8 hours.

4. Turn the heat to HIGH and add the orzo or bowtie pasta. Cover and cook 30 minutes more.

5. Taste before serving. If necessary, reseason with a dash of salt, pepper, and any other flavors that may have cooked out. Serve with grated Parmesan on top, if desired.

them in a glass of water. Store them in your refrigerator. They'll last much longer. This method works for everything except the herbs with woody stems, such as rosemary and thyme. Those can be wrapped up in damp paper towels, placed in plastic zip-top bags and stored in the refrigerator.

$\mathcal{M}$issy's Easy Meatball Minestrone

If you have any of our bread machine cookbooks, you may have noticed that our dogs are very important members of our families, too. While our husbands gave this hearty soup a thumbs up, it was Lois's dog Missy that gave it the final stamp of approval with a big wag of her tail.

1 tablespoon olive oil

1 pound frozen meatballs

1 medium onion, chopped

5 cups beef broth (or 5 cups water and 5 teaspoons beef stock base such as Better than Bouillon)

1 (14½-ounce) can diced tomatoes, Italian-style

1 cup peeled and sliced carrots, about ⅛-inch thick

1 cup sliced celery, about ¼-inch thick

½ cup chopped green pepper

½ teaspoon dried oregano

½ teaspoon dried basil

1 tablespoon chopped fresh Italian parsley

1 cup elbow macaroni

1 (16-ounce) can kidney beans, rinsed and drained

Grated Parmesan cheese as a garnish

SERVES: 6

SLOW COOKER SIZE: 4 quart

PREP TIME: 30 minutes

COOKING TIME: 6 to 8 hours on LOW

Serving Suggestions

Pair this with a light spinach salad and warm bread sticks drizzled with a little garlic butter.

Variations

You can substitute 5 bouillon cubes for the beef stock base.

To speed up and lighten up this recipe, you can omit the olive oil and skip the first two steps.

To "heat up" this recipe, add a dash or two of red pepper flakes.

Tip

When pouring the heated contents of a skillet into the slow cooker pot, we suggest placing the slow cooker pot in

1. In a nonstick skillet, heat the oil over medium heat. Add the meatballs and brown on all sides. Just before they are fully browned, add the onion to the skillet and reduce heat to medium low. Continue cooking until the onions are soft, about 2 more minutes.

2. Add 1 cup of beef broth to the pan, stirring up all browned particles from the bottom of

the pan. Carefully pour contents of skillet into the slow cooker.

3. Add rest of beef broth, tomatoes, carrots, celery, green pepper, oregano, basil, and parsley to the slow cooker. Cover, cook on LOW for 6 to 8 hours.

4. Turn the heat to HIGH. Add the macaroni and kidney beans; stir. Cover and cook about 30 minutes until the macaroni is fully cooked.

5. Taste before serving. If necessary, reseason with a dash of salt, pepper, and any other flavors that may have been diluted during cooking. Serve in soup bowls with grated Parmesan on top.

the sink and pouring the contents of the skillet into it there. If you accidently spill, you'll avoid burning yourself and clean up will be easier.

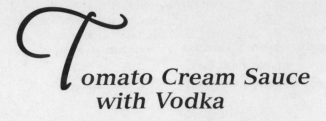omato Cream Sauce with Vodka

Adding vodka makes the tomato flavor pop right out of this pasta sauce. No need to use your most expensive bottle of vodka. An inexpensive brand will do.

2 tablespoons olive oil

½ cup peeled and finely chopped shallots

3 cloves garlic, minced

1 cup vodka

2 (28-ounce) cans crushed tomatoes in puree

1 teaspoon dried oregano

1 teaspoon sugar

Salt and pepper to taste

2 cups heavy cream

1. Heat the oil in a Dutch oven over medium heat. Add the shallots and cook until softened, about 3 minutes. Add the garlic and cook 1 minute more.

2. Stir in the vodka and bring to a boil over medium heat. Boil about 3 minutes until reduced by half.

3. Add remaining ingredients, except the heavy cream. Pour mixture into slow cooker and stir to combine. Cover and cook on LOW for 10 to 12 hours.

4. Just before serving, stir in the heavy cream and heat through about 5 minutes. Taste be-

| YIELD: about 3½ cups |
| SLOW COOKER SIZE: 4 quart |
| PREP TIME: 20 minutes |
| COOKING TIME: 10 to 12 hours on LOW |

Serving Suggestions

Serve over cooked penne pasta with steamed broccoli as an accompaniment. For an elegant touch, top off the meal with a tray of flavorful or imported cheeses and fresh fruit.

Variations

If you don't want to add vodka to this sauce, just substitute ½ cup tomato puree or juice.

To lighten, substitute evaporated skim milk for the cream.

Tip

Shallots are about the size of large pearl onions and have brown skins. They have a more subtle flavor than onions, which makes them perfect for this sauce.

fore serving. If necessary, reseason with a dash of salt, pepper, and any other flavors that may have been diluted during cooking. Serve this over penne pasta, which is the traditional pasta for this dish. Refrigerate or freeze any remaining sauce.

$\mathcal{F}$rijoles Refritos (Refried Beans)
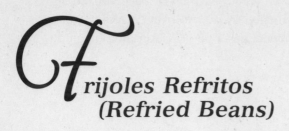

Frijoles are a staple in most Hispanic households. Try these the next time you feel like hosting your own fiesta. This recipe skips the overnight soak. We feel if you're going to the trouble to make frijoles, it's worth making a big pot of them, so we used a 6-quart slow cooker for this recipe. If you have a 4-quart cooker, see "Variations."

2 pounds dry pinto beans, rinsed and picked over

1 large onion, peeled and chopped

1 large clove garlic, peeled and minced

1 teaspoon pepper

2 tablespoons vegetable oil

10 cups water

1 tablespoon salt

½ cup vegetable oil

2 jalapeño, Anaheim, or green bell peppers,
   stemmed, seeded, and minced, optional

½ cup shredded cheddar cheese, optional

½ cup shredded Monterey jack cheese, optional

SERVES: 12

SLOW COOKER SIZE: 6 quart

PREP TIME: 20 minutes total

**COOKING TIME: 7 to 8 hours
on HIGH**

Serving Suggestions

These beans are a good side dish or a filling for tacos, burritos, enchiladas, tamales, tostadas, or fajitas. For easy bean burritos, place about ¾ cup of frijoles in the center of a large flour tortilla. Fold in the sides then roll up into a little package. Heat 2 at a time in the microwave at 50% heat for about 8 to 10 minutes. Serve with guacamole, chunky salsa, shredded cheese, and sour cream.

Variations

Authentic frijoles are fried in lard instead of vegetable oil.

To lighten, reduce the oil to 4 tablespoons and omit step 5.

1. Place beans, onion, garlic, pepper, oil, and water in slow cooker.

2. Cover and cook on HIGH for 7 to 8 hours until the beans are very tender.

3. Drain beans and reserve the cooking liquid. Stir salt into the beans.

4. In a large Dutch oven, heat the oil over medium heat. Add 3 cups of beans and ¼ cup

reserved cooking liquid at a time. Mash with a potato masher or fork to the desired consistency. Repeat this process until all the beans have been mashed. For a creamier consistency, you can mash in more cooking liquid or water at the end.

5. Optional: stir in chili or bell peppers and spread mixture in two 9 × 13-inch baking dishes. Sprinkle grated cheddar and Monterey jack cheese on top and bake in a 350°F oven for 10 minutes until cheese melts.

You can cut the recipe in half and use a 4-quart slow cooker. The beans will be done in 5 to 5½ hours.

 Tip

Adding salt to beans while they cook impedes the softening process.

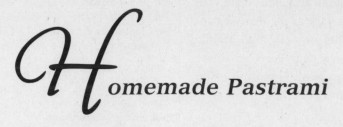 omemade Pastrami

Nothing beats the pastrami sandwiches dished up at your favorite deli, but this recipe is the closest you can come at home.

4 pounds corned beef brisket, trimmed of fat

2 onions, peeled and sliced

2 cloves garlic, peeled and crushed

2 tablespoons pickling spices

1¹/₂ cups water

1 tablespoon coarsely crushed black peppercorns

³/₄ teaspoon freshly grated nutmeg

³/₄ teaspoon ground allspice

1 teaspoon paprika

¹/₂ teaspoon liquid smoke

1. Place brisket, onions, garlic, pickling spice, and water in slow cooker. Cover and cook on LOW 8 to 10 hours.

2. Remove brisket and set aside until cool enough to handle.

3. Preheat the oven to 350°F.

4. In a small bowl, combine the remaining ingredients and thoroughly rub over the entire brisket. Place in a roasting pan and bake for 45 minutes.

5. Remove and let rest 5 to 10 minutes. Brush off most of the rub mixture coating the brisket. Thinly slice on the diagonal or against the grain to serve.

SERVES: 12
SLOW COOKER SIZE: 4 quart
PREP TIME: 15 minutes total
COOKING TIME: 8 to 10 hours on LOW and 45 minutes in the oven

Serving Suggestions

Serve on a good deli rye bread with mustard, and a kosher pickle and a scoop of potato salad.

Variations

You could divide the work on this dish into two days. Cook the brisket the day before or overnight, then bake it in the oven the next day or just before serving.

Tip

To coarsely crush peppercorns, place them in a zip-top plastic bag and pound with a meat mallet or the bottom of a heavy saucepan.

 entil Chili

Serve this chili when you want a low-fat and healthy but filling meal.

1½ cups dry lentils, rinsed

½ cup bulgur

1 onion, chopped

2 cloves garlic, minced

1 large carrot, peeled and grated

1 small green bell pepper, seeded and diced

2 (14-ounce) cans beef or vegetable broth

2 (16-ounce) cans diced tomatoes, undrained

2 tablespoons chili powder

2 teaspoons ground cumin

1 teaspoon oregano

Salt and pepper to taste

OPTIONAL GARNISHES:

crumbled tortilla chips

grated cheddar cheese

diced onions

diced tomatoes

sour cream

1. Place all ingredients in slow cooker and stir to combine. Cover and cook on LOW for 6 to 8 hours.

2. Taste before serving. If necessary, reseason with a dash of salt, pepper, and any other flavors that may have cooked out. Serve hot with optional garnishes, if desired

---

SERVES: 6

SLOW COOKER SIZE: 4 quart

PREP TIME: 15 minutes

COOKING TIME: 6 to 8 hours on LOW

Serving Suggestions

Serve with coleslaw and biscuits.

Serve leftovers the next day as a topper for baked potatoes.

Variations

If you like your chili very spicy, use canned diced tomatoes with jalapeños.

You could substitute 2 cups diced potato for the bulgur during last 3 hours of cooking.

For an even heartier chili, add 1 (15-ounce) can rinsed and drained kidney beans, or 1 cup frozen corn at the end, and heat through.

Tip

To avoid tears while chopping onions, refrigerate the onion beforehand. This is the only method we've found that really works.

$\mathcal{L}$ite Turkey Chili

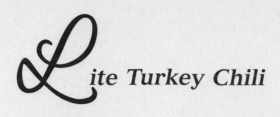

This one's a keeper! You can enjoy this chili without guilt and never miss the calories and fat we've eliminated.

1 tablespoon vegetable oil

¼ teaspoon red pepper flakes, or to taste

1½ pounds ground turkey

1 onion, peeled and chopped

3 tablespoons chili powder

2 teaspoons ground cumin

1 teaspoon ground coriander

Salt and pepper to taste

1 (28-ounce can) crushed tomatoes in puree

1 (1½ pound) butternut squash, peeled, seeded, and cut into ¾-inch cubes

½ green bell pepper, stemmed, seeded, and diced

½ red bell pepper, stemmed, seeded, and diced

1 large carrot, peeled and coarsely grated

1 teaspoon dried oregano

1 (16-ounce) can pinto beans, rinsed and drained

OPTIONAL GARNISHES:

chopped red onions

lite sour cream

chopped fresh cilantro

reduced-fat cheddar cheese, grated

1. Heat the oil in a large nonstick skillet over medium heat. Sprinkle in the red pepper flakes to infuse the oil with their flavor and cook 1 minute.

SERVES: 4

SLOW COOKER SIZE: 4 quart

PREP TIME: 25 minutes

COOKING TIME: 6 to 8 hours on LOW

Serving Suggestions

We like to serve this chili with a wedge of cantaloupe and some saltine crackers or homemade corn bread. For a luscious dessert, try a bowl of fresh strawberries drizzled with a little balsamic vinegar and a dollop of fat-free whipped topping.

Variations

This is a spicy chili. If you like your chili on the mild side, omit the red pepper flakes and reduce the chili powder to 2 tablespoons.

You could easily substitute leftover cooked turkey for the ground. Stir it in at the end.

If you're not a squash lover, you can easily omit it.

And if you're a vegetarian, simply omit the turkey.

2. Add the turkey, onion, chili powder, cumin, coriander, salt and pepper, and cook and stir until the turkey is no longer pink, about 8 minutes. Remove from heat and pour contents of skillet into slow cooker.

3. Add the remaining ingredients, except the beans and any optional garnishes, to slow cooker. Stir to combine; cover and cook on LOW for 6 to 8 hours.

4. Stir in the beans during the last 30 minutes of cooking.

5. Taste before serving. If necessary, reseason with a dash of salt, pepper, and any other seasonings that may have been diluted during cooking. Serve with small bowls of chopped red onion, cilantro, sour cream, and cheese for garnish, if desired.

For a change of pace, vary the type of beans used.

Tip

So many recipes call for chopped onions. To save some time, chop up several onions at once in the food processor then place in zip-top plastic bags and store in the freezer for future use.

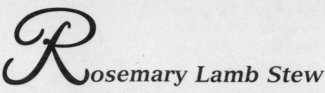

Rosemary Lamb Stew

This flavorful, rustic stew can be combined the night before, refrigerated, and then placed in the slow cooker the next morning. Cook it on a timer while you're at work and you'll be greeted with its wonderful aroma when you walk through the door at night.

8 small red potatoes, quartered

3 large carrots, peeled and cut into 2-inch chunks

2 tablespoons olive oil

2 pounds boneless leg of lamb (see Tip)

8 to 12 pearl onions, peeled

8 to 12 button mushrooms, wiped with damp cloth

3 cloves garlic, minced

2 tablespoons flour

Salt and pepper, to taste

1 (10-ounce) can condensed beef broth

½ cup red wine

2 tablespoons Dijon mustard

1½ cups frozen peas, thawed

1 to 2 tablespoons fresh rosemary, finely chopped

1. Place potatoes and carrots in slow cooker.

2. Heat olive oil in a large Dutch oven over medium-high heat. Add the lamb and brown well, about 5 minutes. Remove with slotted spoon and place in slow cooker.

3. Reduce heat to medium. Add onions, mushrooms, and garlic to the skillet and sauté about three minutes. Remove with slotted spoon and place in slow cooker.

SERVES: 4

SLOW COOKER SIZE: 4 quart

PREP TIME: 45 minutes

COOKING TIME: 6 to 8 hours on LOW

Serving Suggestions

Serve with sliced zucchini squash quickly sautéed in olive oil and minced garlic. Sprinkle with a little freshly grated Parmesan before serving. A dish of pineapple sherbet for dessert would suffice.

Variations

To save time (at the expense of some flavor), skip step 2 and just place all ingredients in slow cooker without browning the meat first.

Also, you can substitute frozen pearl onions for fresh.

You can substitute ¼ cup water for the ½ cup wine.

You can also cook this the day before to allow the flavor to fully develop.

4. To the remaining oil in the Dutch oven, stir in flour, salt and pepper, and cook for about 1 minute. Stir in broth, wine, and mustard, bring to a boil and boil for 1 minute. Pour over ingredients in slow cooker and stir. Cover and cook on LOW for 6 to 8 hours.

5. Stir in peas and rosemary. If necessary, re-season with a dash of salt, pepper, and any other flavors that may have cooked out. Cover and cook on LOW 10 to 15 minutes more until the peas are heated.

Tip

Most legs of lamb we found weighed about 4 pounds. We simply cut one in half and used one half for this recipe and froze the other half for future use.

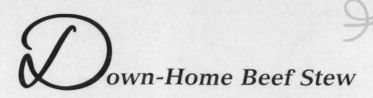

Down-Home Beef Stew

Beef stew ranks right up there with meat loaf and mashed potatoes as the best of the comfort foods. This is Linda's family recipe converted for the slow cooker. The next time you need a soothing meal, try this classic stew.

2 jumbo russet potatoes, peeled and cut into 1-inch cubes

2 large carrots, peeled and cut into 1½-inch chunks

1 medium onion, peeled and quartered

1 tablespoon vegetable oil

2 pounds beef stew meat or boneless chuck steak cut into 1-inch cubes

½ cup flour

1 tablespoon dry onion soup mix

1 tablespoon Worcestershire sauce

1 (14-ounce) can beef or vegetable broth

1 cup water

1 cup frozen peas, thawed

Salt and pepper to taste

SERVES: 4	
SLOW COOKER SIZE: 4 quart	
PREP TIME: 25 minutes	
COOKING TIME: 8 to 10 hours on LOW	

Serving Suggestions

This one-pot meal only calls for a simple salad, maybe a loaf of good sourdough bread, and homemade chocolate chip cookies for dessert.

Variations

To save time (but sacrifice some flavor), skip steps 2 and 3 and just dredge the meat in the flour mixture, then place in slow cooker first.

Tip

Rubber-coated whisks are great for making gravy in nonstick skillets so you don't scratch the surface.

1. Place the potatoes, carrots, and onions in the bottom of the slow cooker.

2. In a large nonstick skillet, heat the oil over medium-high heat. Add the meat and cook until no longer pink. Remove with a slotted spoon and place meat in slow cooker on top of the vegetables.

3. Stir flour and onion soup mix into juices in the skillet. Whisk in the Worcestershire sauce, broth, and water. Bring to boil, and cook until the gravy thickens, breaking up

any large lumps of flour. Pour the gravy over the ingredients in slow cooker.

4. Cover and cook on LOW for 8 to 10 hours. Five minutes before serving, stir in the peas to heat through and season to taste with salt and pepper.

New England Boiled Dinner

The slow cooker is the perfect appliance for cooking corned beef, since the fat-to-lean ratio of brisket is ideal for long braising. Guard those leftovers! It just wouldn't be right if you didn't have enough left for corned beef sandwiches the next day.

1 (3- to-4-pound) flat-cut corned beef brisket, trimmed of fat

Seasoning packet that comes with the corned beef brisket

Water to barely cover brisket, approximately 3 cups

5 medium russet potatoes, peeled and quartered

5 carrots, peeled and cut into 3-inch chunks

2 onions, peeled and quartered

$^{1}/_{2}$ small head of green cabbage, cut into wedges

1. Place corned beef in slow cooker and sprinkle contents of seasoning packet on top, if it came with one.

2. Add water, then add rest of ingredients, except for the cabbage. Cover and cook on LOW for 10 to 12 hours.

3. Add cabbage, pushing it down into the liquid, cover, and cook 30 minutes more.

4. Remove corned beef from liquid, allow to rest for 5 to 10 minutes, then slice on the diagonal and serve on a platter, surrounded by the drained vegetables.

SERVES: 6
SLOW COOKER SIZE: 6 quart
PREP TIME: 20 minutes
COOKING TIME: 10 to 12 hours on LOW

Serving Suggestions

Bring this platter to the table and all you need to add is some chunky applesauce, a jar of Dijon or horseradish mustard, and a loaf of good rye bread.

If you're lucky enough to have leftover meat, nothing beats a simple corned beef sandwich on rye with a schmear of Dijon mustard. Or you could jazz it up a bit and make a Reuben sandwich by toasting the rye bread and adding Thousand Island dressing, sauerkraut, some corned beef, and topping it with a slice of Swiss cheese. Run it under the broiler until the cheese bubbles, top with another slice of toasted rye bread and you have a fabulous sandwich!

And there's always corned beef hash, a delicious breakfast recipe to use up leftovers that may not be in perfect slices.

Variations

If the slow cooker pot is too crowded to cook the cabbage, scoop out about 2 cups of liquid, pour it into a saucepan, and cook cabbage on the stove in the simmering liquid for about 10 minutes until just softened.

Tip

If the corned beef didn't come with a seasoning packet, just toss in a handful of pickling spice, garlic, and a couple of bay leaves.

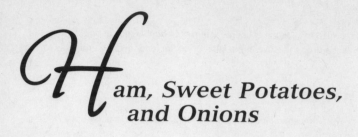 am, Sweet Potatoes, and Onions

If the weather is gloomy, try this colorful, soul satisfying concoction. It will brighten your day!

1 (2-pound) fully-cooked boneless ham or ham steaks

2 pounds (about 4 medium) sweet potatoes, peeled and cut into 1-inch cubes (see Tip)

2 medium Vidalia or other sweet onions, cut into 1-inch pieces

½ cup orange marmalade

2 cloves garlic, peeled and minced

½ teaspoon salt

¼ teaspoon pepper

½ teaspoon dried thyme

1. Trim fat and skin off ham, if desired. Cut into 1-inch cubes.

2. Place all ingredients in slow cooker and stir to combine. Cover and cook on LOW for 6 to 8 hours.

3. Before serving, reseason with a dash or two of salt, pepper, and thyme. Heat through and serve.

SERVES: 6

SLOW COOKER SIZE: 4 quart

PREP TIME: 20 minutes

COOKING TIME: 6 to 8 hours on LOW

Serving Suggestions

This dish is great with a Waldorf salad of chopped apple, chopped celery, walnuts, and a little mayo to bind. Set out a plate of gingersnaps for dessert.

Variations

You could subsitute butternut squash for the sweet potatoes and various herbs for the thyme, such as *herbes de Provence*, rosemary, or parsley.

You could also add a 20-ounce can of pineapple chunks, drained.

Tip

Peel a garlic clove with ease by whacking it with the flat side of a chef's knife. The outer skin slides right off.

Use the dark sweet potatoes often labeled as "yams" in the market.

$\mathcal{M}$arsha's Pork Chops, Potatoes, and Sauerkraut

Sometimes the simplest recipes can be surprisingly flavorful. Many thanks to Linda's good friend Marsha Peterson for suggesting this recipe. It's a keeper!

1 tablespoon oil

4 boneless pork chops, 1-inch thick, center cut

4 large potatoes, peeled and quartered

1 (32-ounce) can, bottle, or bag of sauerkraut

Salt and pepper to taste

SERVES: 4
SLOW COOKER SIZE: 4½ quart
PREP TIME: 20 minutes
COOKING TIME: 6 to 8 hours on LOW

1. In a large nonstick skillet, heat the oil over medium-high heat until hot but not smoking. Add the pork chops and lightly brown both sides, about 5 minutes per side.

2. Place potatoes in slow cooker, add pork chops, then cover with sauerkraut. Cover and cook on LOW for 6 to 8 hours.

3. Serve, adding salt and pepper to taste.

Serving Suggestions

Serve with warm applesauce, a good mustard, and a colorful vegetable. If the calorie gods allow, a slice of carrot cake for dessert would be delish!

Variations

To speed up the process, omit step 1.

For added flavor, sprinkle a little brown sugar over the sauerkraut or drizzle some maple syrup over the chops before cooking.

Tip

If you prefer your sauerkraut milder, rinse and drain well before adding to the slow cooker.

Carnitas

This tasty shredded pork makes an easy homemade filling for tacos, burritos, tostadas, enchiladas or tamales. It was a big hit in our homes; even our finicky dogs sat up and took notice when we lifted the lid on this dish.

1 (3-pound) pork shoulder, cross rib, or Boston butt roast, well trimmed of fat

1 (16-ounce) jar very flavorful salsa

1. Place ingredients in slow cooker, cover, and cook on LOW for 10 to 12 hours, until falling apart.

2. Remove roast from slow cooker and place in a 9 × 13-inch pan or dish. Remove any remaining fat, then shred meat well with two forks. Return shredded meat to slow cooker and stir to coat well with sauce. Use right away or freeze in zip-top freezer bags for future use.

SERVES: 12
SLOW COOKER SIZE: 4 quart
PREP TIME: 5 minutes
COOKING TIME: 10 to 12 hours on LOW

Serving Suggestions

You can set this on a buffet with a basket of crisp taco shells or warm flour tortillas, and supply garnishes, like chopped tomatoes, shredded lettuce, refried beans, chopped onion, fresh cilantro, guacamole, sour cream, grated cheese, chopped olives, diced chiles, salsa, hot sauce, etc. Let your guests build their own tacos or burritos. Add a green salad or bowl of fruit and Spanish rice.

Variations

For more flavor, heat a little vegetable oil in a Dutch oven over medium-high heat and brown the meat well on all sides first.

Tip

Once the roast has been removed from the slow cooker, there's quite a bit of sauce in the pot. Use half of it as part of the liquid to cook Spanish rice.

$\mathcal{P}$oulet Provençal

Celebrate the flavors of southern France with this hearty chicken dish.

10 small red potatoes, unpeeled and quartered

1 large onion, peeled and cut into quarters then sliced

4 cloves garlic, minced

1 cup pitted Niçoise olives

1 tablespoon herbes de Provence

Salt and pepper, to taste

1 tablespoon olive oil

About 3 pounds of chicken thighs or drumsticks, or a combination of both

1. Place first 6 ingredients in slow cooker in order listed.

2. In a large nonstick skillet over medium-high heat, heat the olive oil and sauté chicken in batches until brown on all sides, about 10 minutes. Pour contents of skillet over vegetables in slow cooker.

3. Cover and cook on LOW for 6 to 8 hours.

4. Taste before serving. If necessary, reseason with a dash of salt, pepper, and any other flavors that may have cooked out.

SERVES: 4

SLOW COOKER SIZE: 6 quart

PREP TIME: 35 minutes

COOKING TIME: 6 to 8 hours on LOW

Serving Suggestions

For an easy salad, toss together cherry tomatoes, crumbled feta cheese, chopped red onion, chopped fresh basil, oregano, or parsley and a good vinaigrette. Serve with some garlic bread, sprinkled with a little freshly grated Parmesan cheese and put under the broiler until the cheese bubbles.

Variations

To save time (but sacrifice some flavor), skip step 2 and place chicken in bottom of slow cooker without browning first. Drizzle olive oil over vegetables.

Tip

Herbes de Provence is a dry blend of several herbs, such as basil, rosemary, marjoram, lavender, savory, thyme.

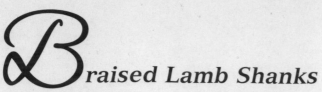

Braised Lamb Shanks

This is one of Lois's favorite meals. Lamb shanks and slow cookers are perfect partners. Start this recipe the night before for the best flavor.

1 cup dry red wine

1 cup beef broth

3 tablespoons Dijon mustard

4 sprigs fresh thyme, minced

2 sprigs fresh rosemary leaves, minced

1 lemon, sliced

6 large cloves garlic, cut in half

Salt and pepper, to taste

4 lamb shanks, about 12 ounces each, trimmed of fat

1 tablespoon olive oil

1 large onion, peeleed and cut into chunks

2 carrots, peeled and cut into chunks

2 stalks celery, cut into chunks

2 bay leaves

SERVES: 4
SLOW COOKER SIZE: 4 quart
PREP TIME: 25 minutes
COOKING TIME: 10 to 12 hours on LOW

Serving Suggestions

For an authentic Mediterranean meal, serve these over cooked cannellini beans. Cook a few pieces of bacon, drain and crumble over the beans. Sauté 2 cloves minced garlic in bacon grease then stir in a can of cannellini beans that have been rinsed and drained. Stir in a tablespoon of tomato paste and a spoonful or two of the lamb shank cooking liquid. Heat through and serve with crumbled bacon on top. Finish the meal with a cold slice of melon.

Variations

To save time (but sacrifice some flavor), skip steps 2 and 3 and just place rest of ingredients in slow cooker without browning the meat first.

1. The night before, place the first 8 ingredients in a large zip-top bag and add the lamb shanks. Refrigerate overnight.

2. The next morning, remove the lamb shanks and drain on paper towels, reserving the marinade.

3. Heat the oil in a large nonstick skillet over medium-high heat. Carefully place the lamb shanks in the oil and brown well on all sides. Remove and place in the slow cooker in the marinade.

4. Add the onion, carrots, celery, and bay leaves. Cover and cook on LOW for 10 to 12 hours until the meat is falling off the bone.

5. To serve, remove the lamb shanks and place on a platter. Discard the bay leaves. With a slotted spoon, remove the vegetables and spread over lamb shanks. Strain the leftover juices and pour a little over all.

Tip

To strip the fresh thyme and rosemary off the woody stems, just hold the top and run your fingers down the stem. The leaves will peel off with ease.

$\mathcal{G}$inger's Five-Spice Chicken

When the call went out for favorite slow cooker recipes at the Bernardo Heights Middle School, where Linda works, Ginger Riggs was the first to respond with a quick and easy chicken recipe that inspired this version. Wow, does it smell great as it cooks!

1 (3- to 3½-pound) whole chicken
½ cup low-salt soy sauce or teriyaki marinade
½ cup dry sherry or rice wine
½ cup Chinese plum sauce or hoisin sauce
2 cloves garlic, minced
1½ teaspoons grated fresh ginger root
1 teaspoon Chinese five-spice powder

1. Place chicken in slow cooker.

2. In a medium bowl, combine the remaining ingredients and pour over chicken.

3. Cover and cook on LOW for 4 to 6 hours. If you're home, turn the chicken over after 2 hours.

4. To serve, cut up chicken and serve with some sauce on the side.

SERVES: 4

SLOW COOKER SIZE: 4 quart

PREP TIME: 5 minutes

COOKING TIME: 4 to 6 hours on LOW

Serving Suggestions

Serve over steamed white or brown rice with some stir-fried snow peas. Orange sherbet for dessert would be a perfect, crisp ending to this meal. Any leftover chicken would be great added to a Chinese chicken salad or shredded over a Caesar salad.

Variations

You can substitute bone-in chicken pieces for the whole chicken.

You can substitute reduced-salt chicken broth, or apple juice, for the wine.

Try substituting various bottled marinades for the soy sauce, plum sauce, ginger, and five-spice powder.

Before placing the chicken in the slow cooker, be sure to remove the giblets, heart, etc. that have been packaged inside the cavity.

Some light soy sauces have nearly as much sodium as regular soy sauce, so look for soy sauces specifically labelled "less sodium."

Turkey Breast with Ginger-Orange Glaze

It's easy to find turkey breast at the supermarket Tuesdays, so you don't have to wait until Thanksgiving to enjoy turkey. Orange and ginger flavors perk up this simple dish.

½ cup orange marmalade

1 tablespoon peeled and grated fresh ginger

1 clove garlic, minced

½ teaspoon dried thyme

Salt and pepper to taste

¼ cup freshly squeezed orange juice

1 (3- to 3½-pound) bone-in turkey breast

FOR OPTIONAL SAUCE:

2 tablespoons water

1 tablespoon cornstarch

¾ teaspoon poultry seasoning

¾ teaspoon *herbes de Provence*

Salt and pepper to taste

1 tablespoon sherry, optional

2 tablespoons butter

1. In a bowl, combine the marmalade, ginger, garlic, thyme and salt and pepper to taste.

2. Pour orange juice in bottom of slow cooker and place the turkey breast skin side up on top. Brush orange glaze on turkey breast.

3. Cover and cook on LOW for 4 to 5 hours. For best results, insert an instant-read ther-

SERVES: 4

SLOW COOKER SIZE: 4½ quart

PREP TIME: 10 minutes

COOKING TIME: 4 to 5 hours on LOW

Serving Suggestions

This would be wonderful sliced and served on top of Savory Bread Stuffing (see page 228) made the day before or in a second slow cooker. Add fresh stalks of roasted asparagus to complete the meal. Break off the woody ends of each stalk of asparagus, marinate asparagus in a balsamic vinaigrette dressing briefly or for several hours, then grill on a hot grill until tender or place under the broiler for a few minutes on each side until browned.

For a simpler meal, serve the turkey breast with a packaged wild rice blend and baked yams, or steamed butternut squash.

Variations

If you have time, try brining the turkey breast first in your slow

mometer into the thickest part of the meat (avoid touching the bone). It will be done when it reaches 165°F. Remove turkey breast and keep warm.

4. For the sauce, pour the contents of the slow cooker into a saucepan over MEDIUM heat. In a small bowl, stir together water and cornstarch. Pour into saucepan and whisk together until mixture comes to a boil. Reduce heat to LOW, stir in herbs, salt and pepper, and sherry. Then whisk in the butter until melted.

cooker liner. Stir together 3 quarts water, 3/4 cup kosher salt, and 3/4 cup sugar. Place turkey breast in brine, cover, and refrigerate 6 hours or overnight. Remove, rinse, and pat dry; discard the brine. This produces a wonderfully tender, juicy breast of turkey.

 Tip

Whenever you add cornstarch to a sauce to thicken it, mix it first with a little liquid. Then once added, do not overcook the sauce. If allowed to boil too long, the cornstarch will break down and lose its thickening power.

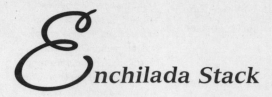nchilada Stack

Here's a surefire winner for your next potluck supper.

1½ pounds ground beef

1 onion, chopped

1 teaspoon chili powder

¼ teaspoon cayenne pepper

1 (19-ounce) can enchilada sauce

1 dozen corn tortillas

1 cup (4 ounces) shredded cheddar cheese

1 cup (4 ounces) shredded Monterey jack cheese

1 (3.8-ounce) can sliced black olives, drained

Sour cream

Guacamole (recipe follows)

1. In a large nonstick skillet over medium heat, sauté ground beef and onions until no pink remains. Remove from heat and stir in chili powder and cayenne. Set aside.

2. Place 3 tablespoons of enchilada sauce in bottom of slow cooker. Place 3 tortillas on top of sauce, then ¼ of hamburger mixture, ¼ of shredded cheeses, ¼ of olives, and ¼ of remaining enchilada sauce. Repeat layers 3 more times, ending with sauce.

3. Cover and cook on LOW for 6 to 8 hours. To serve, scoop down to the bottom for each serving and top with sour cream and guacamole.

SERVES: 4
SLOW COOKER SIZE: 4 quart
PREP TIME: 30 minutes
COOKING TIME: 6 to 8 hours on LOW

Serving Suggestions

Serve with a green salad topped with some drained mandarin oranges, chopped red onion, and tossed with poppy seed dressing.

For our favorite light dessert, gently stir a 20-ounce can of pineapple chunks (undrained) into a packaged angel food cake mix. Pour into a greased bundt pan and bake at 350°F for 40 minutes. Cool 10 minutes, then turn out. Serve with sliced fresh strawberries or any fresh fruit of choice.

Variations

To lighten the dish, reduce beef to 1 pound, or substitute ground turkey for the ground beef. Substitute reduced-fat cheddar cheese and omit the jack cheese. Go easy on the guacamole and choose light sour cream instead of regular.

GUACAMOLE

1 large, ripe avocado

2–3 teaspoons fresh lemon juice

1/4 teaspoon salt

2 tablespoons onion, finely chopped

To make guacamole, remove the peel and pit from the avocado. In a shallow dish, mash the avocado well with a fork. Sprinkle the lemon juice and salt over the avocado. Add onion and mix all together well with a fork. This is a very simple guacamole recipe to which you can add chopped tomatoes, chopped cilantro or diced chiles as desired.

Tip

If transporting a slow cooker meal to a potluck and you don't have an insulated carrier, just wrap it well in newspaper and a couple of beach towels. It will stay warm for quite a while.

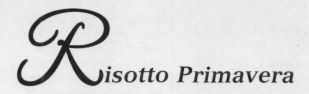isotto Primavera

This colorful, nutritious risotto is the perfect side dish for grilled fish or chicken, but can easily become a fix-it-and-forget-it main course with the addition of some shrimp or leftover cooked meat in the final minutes. Note that the cooking time for this no-hassle risotto is only 1½ hours on HIGH.

1 tablespoon olive oil

1 large onion, peeled and chopped

1 large carrot, peeled and coarsely shredded

1 cup uncooked arborio rice

1 (14-ounce) can chicken broth

½ cup dry white wine

¼ teaspoon salt

½ teaspoon pepper

1 cup frozen peas, thawed

1 small red bell pepper, stemmed, seeded and
   chopped

Juice of ½ lemon

1 cup warm water

¼ cup (1 ounce) freshly grated Parmesan cheese

1 tablespoon fresh thyme leaves or 1 teaspoon
   dried thyme

SERVES: 4 as a main dish or 6 as a side dish

SLOW COOKER SIZE: 4 quart

PREP TIME: 15 minutes

COOKING TIME: 1½ hours on HIGH

Serving Suggestions

Serve as a side dish with grilled fish and a dinner salad, or cut up about ¾ pound raw shrimp or various cooked meats and stir into the risotto at the end for a complete meal in one pot. (Don't worry about the shrimp not cooking through. The risotto will be so hot that the small pieces of shrimp will cook immediately.)

Variations

You can substitute ½ cup more chicken broth for the wine.

With an attention to color combinations, you can add or substitute various other vegetables for the ones listed. Grate or chop finely so they will cook quickly.

1. In a skillet over medium heat, sauté the onion in the olive oil until softened, about 4 minutes.

2. Place onions, carrot, rice, broth, wine, salt and pepper into slow cooker and stir to combine. Cover and cook on HIGH for 1½ hours.

3. Gently stir in peas, red pepper, lemon juice, warm water, cheese, and thyme. Cover and cook about 5 minutes more until heated through. Turn off the heat and serve.

Regular white long grain rice will not work as a substitute for arborio rice in this recipe.

*S*low Cooker "Fried" Rice

Sometimes, we like to use the slow cooker just to warm up leftovers. Here's a recipe that uses leftover cooked rice and anything else you want to throw in to create a no-fuss entree. Our favorite addition is chopped cha-siu (Chinese barbequed pork). Look for it at your nearest Chinese market.

2 tablspoons butter or cooking oil spray

3 eggs, lightly beaten

6 cups leftover cooked rice, chilled

1½ cups cooked and chopped leftover fish, meat, or poultry, such as shrimp, bacon, sausage, ham, or barbequed chicken

1 cup frozen peas, rinsed under hot water to thaw

1 cup finely grated carrot

½ cup chopped green onion

2 tablespoon soy sauce

1. Generously butter or spray the bottom of the slow cooker pot.

2. Pour the lightly beaten eggs into the slow cooker

3. In a bowl, combine the rest of the ingredients. Pour into the slow cooker on top of the eggs but DO NOT stir to combine.

4. Cover and cook on HIGH for 1 hour. Stir well, cover, and cook another ½ hour on HIGH, if not completely warmed throughout.

SERVES: 4
Slow cooker size: 4 quart
Prep time: 20 minutes
Cooking time: 1 to 1½ hours on HIGH

Serving Suggestions

To stay with the no-fuss theme, serve a relish tray of packaged, precut veggies with a bowl of fat-free dressing for dipping as an appetizer. If you really want to have some family fun with this meal, remove all silverware and serve the rice in purchased Chinese take out containers with chopsticks. (You can find them at restaurant supply stores or your nearest Chinese market or restaurant.) For dessert, what else? Fortune cookies, of course!

Variations

The variations to this dish are endless. It's the perfect Monday night meal for using up weekend leftovers. The only ingredient you can't alter is the chilled rice.

The key to perfect fried rice, whether done in a wok or crock, is to start with cold cooked rice.

eep-Dish Dinner

For years, Linda made this dish in a skillet, but it works very well in the slow cooker, too.

1 pound ground beef

½ cup chopped onion

4 large potatoes, peeled and sliced ¼-inch thick

Salt and pepper to taste

1 (16-ounce) can green beans, well-drained
  (or substitute frozen green beans)

1 (10-ounce) can cream of mushroom soup

1. Combine the ground beef and chopped onion. Gently shape into 3 or 4 plump patties. In a large nonstick skillet over MEDIUM-HIGH heat, brown the patties well on both sides for about 10 minutes.

2. Meanwhile, place the sliced potatoes in the bottom of the slow cooker and season with salt and pepper. Then add the green beans and soup.

3. When browned, add the burgers and pan juices on top. Cover and cook on LOW 6 to 8 hours. If you're home, after 3 or 4 hours, remove burgers and stir potatoes to coat with the gravy. Replace burgers on top of the potatoes and continue cooking.

SERVES: 3 or 4

SLOW COOKER SIZE: 4 quart

PREP TIME: 20 minutes

COOKING TIME: 6 to 8 hours on LOW

Serving Suggestions

For a simple salad, serve a small wedge of cabbage sprinkled with a little salt. Keep dessert easy too, by offering a bowl of seedless red grapes and small cups of prepared tapioca pudding.

Variations

To speed up preparation, scrub but do not peel potatoes.

You could substitute cream of tomato soup for the mushroom soup and your vegetable of choice for the green beans.

Tip

Slice the potatoes all the same thickness so they'll cook to the same degree of doneness.

Southern-Style Green Beans

We love green beans just about any way they can be cooked. Here's a slow-cooked method that adds a down-home flavor to this great vegetable.

6 slices hickory-smoked bacon, diced

1½ pounds fresh green beans, washed, trimmed, cut into 3-inch pieces

6 red potatoes, unpeeled and quartered

1 teaspoon sugar

½ cup chopped onion

1 clove garlic, minced

Salt and pepper to taste

1. In a nonstick skillet, cook the bacon until crisp.

2. Meanwhile, place the rest of the ingredients in slow cooker. Add the bacon and drippings from the skillet to the pot; stir to combine. Cover and cook on LOW for 6 to 8 hours.

3. Taste before serving. If necessary, reseason with a little more salt and pepper

SERVES: 4

SLOW COOKER SIZE: 4 quart

PREP TIME: 30 min

COOKING TIME: 6 to 8 hours on LOW

Serving Suggestions

Thread some marinated cubes of beef or chicken on skewers with cherry tomatoes or green peppers and onions, cook them on the grill, and in no time you'll have a great main dish to complement these beans. How about a small piece of key lime pie for dessert?

Variations

To lighten, use only 3 strips of bacon and discard all but 2 teaspoons bacon grease. (And if you need to forego the key lime pie, try some key lime–flavored yogurt topped with crumbled graham crackers.)

To speed up, use canned or frozen green beans and cook 2 to 3 hours.

Tip

If using bamboo skewers for the shish kebabs, soak them first in water for at least 30 minutes to prevent them from burning on the grill.

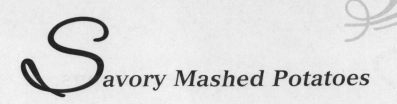

Savory Mashed Potatoes

Here's a new twist on plain mashed potatoes. Mix and match the cheeses and herbs to your liking.

6 large russet potatoes, peeled and quartered

1 cup chicken or vegetable broth

Salt and pepper to taste

1 cup (4 ounces) shredded or crumbled cheese, such as smoked gouda, feta, blue cheese, Swiss, jalapeño pepper jack cheese, or cream cheese

2 tablespoons chopped fresh herbs, such as chives, parsley, oregano, cilantro, dill, or rosemary

¼ cup butter or margarine, optional

1. Place the potatoes, broth, salt and pepper in slow cooker and stir to combine. Cover and cook on LOW for 6 to 8 hours, until the potatoes are fork-tender. If you are home, stir the potatoes once or twice during the first hour to prevent dark spots from forming.

2. Mash by hand with a potato masher. Then stir in cheese, fresh herbs, and butter, if desired. Season to taste with more salt and pepper, if needed.

   SUGGESTED COMBINATIONS:
   smoked gouda and parsley
   feta and oregano
   blue cheese and rosemary
   Swiss cheese and dill

SERVES: 6

SLOW COOKER SIZE: 4 quart

PREP TIME: 15 minutes

COOKING TIME: 6 to 8 hours on LOW

Serving Suggestions

Serve with a grilled steak and fresh or frozen corn on the cob.

Variations

To lighten this recipe, reduce the cheese to ½ cup, or use a reduced-fat version. You can also omit the butter.

To speed up preparation, scrub the potatoes well but do not peel. Then just lightly mash when done and serve as smashed potatoes.

These potatoes are even tastier the next day, rewarmed. The flavors will be more fully developed.

jalapeño pepper jack cheese and cilantro
cream cheese and chives
Parmesan and oregano

Tip

Some cheeses—like blue and feta—are more pungent than others. You may prefer to use less than 1 cup of them for a milder flavor. Taste test after adding ½ cup, to determine how much cheese you want to add.

Celia's Freezable Applesauce

For years, Linda's freezer was well stocked with the wonderful applesauce her Aunt Celia used to make with hand-picked Gravenstein apples. Now Linda uses the slow cooker and her aunt's recipe to recreate those happy memories.

12 apples (about 4 pounds—enough to fill pot ³⁄₄ full), peeled, cored and quartered. Use Gravenstein, Gala, Granny Smith, Macintosh, Cortland, or Fuji apples

¹⁄₂ to 1 cup sugar, depending on the sweetness of the apples

1. Place apples in slow cooker. Cover and cook on LOW for 5 to 6 hours, or on HIGH for 2¹⁄₂ to 3 hours.

2. Stir in sugar. Puree with an immersion blender or potato masher to desired consistency, being careful not to splash yourself.

3. Cool and pour into freezer containers for storage.

SERVES: 6 (makes 1 quart)

SLOW COOKER SIZE: 4 quart

PREP TIME: 30 minutes

COOKING TIME: 5 to 6 hours on LOW or 2¹⁄₂ to 3 hours on HIGH

Serving Suggestions

Serve cold as a healthy snack or warm with pork tenderloin or pork roast. It's also a great topping for potato pancakes or warm gingerbread.

Variations

To lighten, omit the sugar altogether if your apples aren't too tart. If you use a very sweet apple, add about 1 tablespoon lemon juice to cut the sweetness.

For spiced applesauce, stir in 1 teaspoon ground cinnamon, 1 teaspoon ground cloves, and a dash of freshly ground nutmeg, during the last hour of cooking. Another option: omit the sugar and stir in ³⁄₄ to 1 cup cinnamon red hot candies during the last hour of cooking.

If you make applesauce or other apple desserts frequently, consider investing in one of those nifty apple peelers that attach to your countertop. It peels, cores, and slices apples, all with just a few cranks of the handle.

$\mathcal{P}$ineapple Upside-down Carrot Cake

A packaged cake mix means this impressive dessert is also quick and easy to put together.

1 tablespoon butter

¼ cup butter or margarine, melted

1 cup brown sugar

1 (8-ounce) can pineapple slices, drained

1 (10-ounce) jar maraschino cherries, drained, with stems removed

1 (18-ounce) box carrot cake mix

1 cup water

½ cup oil

3 eggs

1. Butter the bottom and sides of slow cooker.

2. In a small bowl, combine the ¼ cup melted butter and brown sugar. Spread in bottom of slow cooker.

3. Place pineapple slices on top of sugar mixture and scatter cherries in open spaces.

4. In a bowl, combine the cake mix, water, oil, and eggs. Pour batter over pineapple, DO NOT STIR. Cover and cook on LOW for 4 to 5 hours, until it tests done in the center with a toothpick.

SERVES: 8

SLOW COOKER SIZE: 4 quart

PREP TIME: 20 minutes

COOKING TIME: 4 to 5 hours on LOW

Serving Suggestions

Serve with a dollop of frozen whipped topping, or some extra fresh or canned pineapple on the side.

Variations

You could add ½ cup chopped nuts, shredded coconut, or raisins to the cake batter.

Also, you can vary the cake mix. Try spice, yellow, or white cake, using the ingredients listed on the box to replace the water, oil, and eggs in this recipe.

Tip

If your package of brown sugar is old and the sugar has turned brick hard, simply microwave it briefly until you can break it apart with a fork.

5. Remove pot from slow cooker and allow cake to cool for 10 minutes. Run a thin rubber spatula around the outside of the cake to loosen it. Place a large plate on top and carefully invert the cake onto the serving plate. Serve warm or at room temperature.

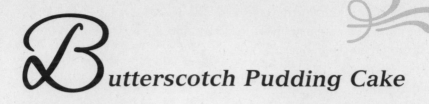

Butterscotch Pudding Cake

Though the pudding is poured on the top of the cake in the beginning, when done it will end up on the bottom. Serve this gooey cake while it's still warm and stand back to wait for the "oohs" and "ahs."

1 tablespoon butter or cooking oil spray

CAKE:

2½ cups flour

1 cup dark brown sugar

1 tablespoon baking powder

1 teaspoon salt

1 (12-ounce package) butterscotch chips

1½ cups milk

½ cup butter or margarine, melted

2 teaspoons vanilla

PUDDING:

1 (3½-ounce) package butterscotch pudding mix

2 cups boiling water

Whipped cream or Cool Whip

1. Butter or spray the bottom and sides of the slow cooker pot.

2. In a bowl, stir together the flour, brown sugar, baking powder, salt, and butterscotch chips. Stir in milk, melted butter, and vanilla. Pour batter into slow cooker.

3. In a separate bowl, combine pudding mix and boiling water; whisk until well blended. Slowly pour over cake batter; *do not mix.*

SERVES: 4

SLOW COOKER SIZE: 4 quart

PREP TIME: 20 minutes

COOKING TIME: 4 to 5 hours on LOW

Serving Suggestions

This scrumptious dessert goes well with a light meal, such as grilled chicken and a green vegetable.

Variations

You can use other puddings in this recipe, such as vanilla or banana.

Tip

Always choose unsalted butter for the freshest flavor.

Cover and cook on LOW for 4 to 5 hours, until the cake is set around the edges. (It will not set completely in the center.)

4. Serve warm directly from the cooker with whipped cream, scooping down to the pudding on the bottom for each serving.

Summer

Summer

Up, Up, and Away Artichoke Dip

Mi Amigo's Red-Hot Snack Mix

Sweet-and-Sour Meatballs

Green Chili Eggs

Blueberry Strata

Cioppino

Peach Butter

Picnic Beans

Italian Beef Sandwiches

Easy Overnight BBQ Beef or Pork
Sandwiches

Kielbasa-and-Lentil Stew

Round Steak Supper

Vegetable Chili

Slow-Cooked Jambalaya

Tamera's Pot Roast and Potatoes

Oriental Flank Steak

Osso Buco

Orange-Glazed Pork Chops

Debbie's Lamb Curry and Rice

Polynesian Chicken

Lemon-Lime Chicken

Viva el Pollo!

Beef-and-Pasta Pot

Bulgur Pilaf

A Pot of Veggies

Garlic Potato Chunks

Balsamic Glazed Carrots

Upside-down Peach Cobbler

Piña Colada Bread Pudding with
Rum Sauce

Lemon Pudding Cake

Fresh Plum Delight

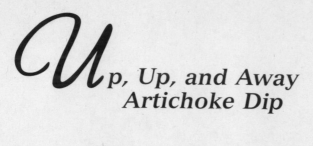p, Up, and Away
Artichoke Dip

Years ago, Linda's daughter Shayna took a hot air balloon ride. When everyone was back on the ground safe and sound, the ballroom company treated everyone to Champagne and this delectable warm dip, served with a variety of crackers. We've had several artichoke dips since, but this one still remains the favorite.

1 (13.5-ounce) can or jar of marinated artichoke
   hearts, well drained and chopped

2 cups light mayonnaise

1 (8-ounce) package cream cheese, cut up

1½ cups (6 ounces) freshly grated Parmesan
   cheese

2 cloves garlic, peeled and minced

½ teaspoon dried dill

½ teaspoon white pepper

1. Place all ingredients in slow cooker and stir well to combine.

2. Cover and cook on HIGH for 1 hour or on LOW for 2 hours. Turn the heat to LOW and serve warm directly from the slow cooker with hearty crackers.

SERVES: 12

SLOW COOKER SIZE: 1½ quart

PREP TIME: 15 minutes

COOKING TIME: 1 hour on HIGH or 2 hours on LOW

Serving Suggestions

Serve this warm dip with hearty, thick crackers, such as Triscuits, that will stand up to dipping.

Variations

You could lighten this dip up just a little by using reduced-fat cream cheese and plain artichoke hearts, not marinated in oil.

Tip

Try using a microplane for faster cheese grating. Visit your local kitchen supply store or www.microplane.com for more information on this unique kitchen tool.

Mi Amigo's Red-Hot Snack Mix

This recipe was inspired by a recent trip to New Mexico, where many people hang strands of dried chili peppers outside their doorways for good luck. A few of those little red chilies really heat up this dish—maybe they'll bring you good luck, too!

4 cups dry-roasted peanuts, salted or unsalted

1 cup shelled sunflower seeds

1 tablespoon vegetable oil

1 teaspoon hot sauce, such as Tabasco

4 small New Mexico, California, or Thai dried red
  chili peppers, or to taste

½ teaspoon garlic powder

2 teaspoons chili powder

½ teaspoon salt, optional

Place all ingredients in slow cooker and stir well to thoroughly coat with seasonings. Cover and cook on HIGH for 1½ hours. Pour onto a large baking sheet to cool. Discard red chili peppers. Store in an airtight container.

SERVES: 10

SLOW COOKER SIZE:
1½ quart

PREP TIME: 10 minutes

COOKING TIME: 1½ hours
on HIGH

Serving Suggestions

You'll definitely need a frosty beverage in hand before you start munching on this salty snack.

Variations

You can substitute quite a few ingredients for the nuts or seeds in this dish, such as little pretzels, puffy cereals, goldfish crackers, or a variety of plain snack mixes.

Tip

Check the Mexican or Asian ingredient sections of your market for packages of the dried red chilis.

Sweet-and-Sour Meatballs

This recipe may date us, because it's a classic from the early '60s, but it never fails to be a crowd-pleasing appetizer. If you've never tried it, now's your chance!

2 tablespoons oil

2 pounds frozen precooked meatballs, defrosted

1 cup (12-ounce jar) chili sauce

1 cup grape jelly

1. In a large skillet, sauté the meatballs in the oil in two batches until browned. Drain.

2. Place the chili sauce and grape jelly in slow cooker and stir to combine. Then stir in the meatballs. Cover and cook on LOW for 4 to 6 hours or on HIGH for 2 to 3 hours.

SERVES: 8

SLOW COOKER SIZE: 4 quart

PREP TIME: 10 minutes

COOKING TIME: 4 to 6 hours on LOW or 2 to 3 hours on HIGH

Serving Suggestions

For an appetizer, serve directly from the slow cooker, set on WARM or LOW. Have plenty of toothpicks nearby.

You could also serve these for dinner with fried rice or noodles.

Variations

To lighten this recipe or if you're pressed for time, skip step 1, omit the oil, and use a low-sugar jam.

Tip

When browning any meats, it's best not to crowd the pan. If too crowded, items tend to steam rather than brown.

reen Chili Eggs

Try this at your next potluck brunch or casual get-together. It will easily serve eight hungry people. If you need it first thing in the morning, set it on a timer to cook during the night.

1 tablespoon butter or cooking oil spray

12 soft corn tortillas, torn into bite-size pieces

1 (7-ounce) can of diced green chilis, drained

1 pound Monterey jack cheese, grated

12 eggs

1 (16-ounce) container sour cream

Salt and pepper to taste

1. Butter or spray the bottom and sides of slow cooker pot.

2. Scatter half of the tortilla pieces in the bottom of the pot. Sprinkle half of the chilis and half of the cheese on top. Repeat the layers.

3. In a bowl, whisk together eggs, sour cream, salt and pepper to taste. Pour over contents in slow cooker.

4. Cover and cook on LOW heat for 4 to 5 hours until the eggs are completely set. Serve warm.

SERVES: 8

SLOW COOKER SIZE: 4 quart

PREP TIME: 15 minutes

COOKING TIME: 4 to 5 hours on LOW

Serving Suggestions

Set out a plate of sliced cantaloupe, bowls of salsa and diced avocados, a basket of warm muffins, and a pitcher of mimosas for sipping, then let your guests help themselves.

Variations

To lighten, substitute 2 cups of Egg Beaters for 8 of the eggs, light sour cream, and reduced-fat jack cheese.

For a large crowd, increase this recipe by half and prepare it in a 6-quart slow cooker, cooking for 5 to 6 hours.

Tip

When you remove the lid, if moisture has gathered on top of the eggs, just run a rubber spatula around the inside of the pot, and the juices will sink to the bottom.

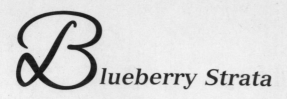lueberry Strata

Celebrate spring with your friends by treating them to this simple brunch dish that cooks while you sleep.

1 tablespoon butter or cooking oil spray

1 (1-pound) loaf of a hearty bread, such as French or Italian, cut into ½-inch cubes (about 12 cups)

1 (8-ounce) package cream cheese, cut into very small cubes

1 cup fresh or frozen blueberries

12 eggs

¼ cup maple syrup

1 cup milk

½ teaspoon salt

Blueberry or maple syrup

1. The morning before serving, butter or spray the bottom and sides of the slow cooker pot.

2. Place half of the bread into the slow cooker.

3. Sprinkle half of the cream cheese cubes and berries over the bread.

4. Repeat the layers and press down slightly.

5. In a bowl, whisk together the eggs, ¼ cup maple syrup, milk, and salt. Pour over the layered bread.

SERVES: 6

SLOW COOKER SIZE: 4 quart

PREP TIME: 25 minutes

COOKING TIME: 5 to 6 hours on LOW

Serving Suggestions

Serve with cooked sausages or Canadian bacon, pineapple spears, and freshly squeezed orange juice.

Variations

To lighten this recipe, use reduced-fat cream cheese, 4 whole eggs plus 2 cups of Egg Beaters, and 1% milk.

Tip

Once opened, maple syrup should be stored in the refrgerator or freezer. If it begins to crystalize, simply heat it in a saucepan or in the microwave. Or if a harmless mold forms on the top, just bring it to a boil and strain through a cheesecloth.

6. Cover and refrigerate all day (about 12 hours). Using a timer to delay the start of cooking for two hours, cook on LOW during the night for 5 to 6 hours.

7. Serve in the morning with warm syrup.

Cioppino

This Italian fish stew is rather costly to make, but we've included it because it's so delicious and a special dish to serve family and friends for a festive occasion. It's our favorite dish for an intimate dinner party, if you plan to linger at the table for hours. The list of ingredients is rather daunting, but you'll find that if you set everything out on the counter at the beginning (except the fish), the whole thing will take a mere 15 minutes to prepare.

¼ cup extra-virgin olive oil

1 small white onion, peeled and chopped

½ cup green pepper, stemmed, seeded, and chopped

1 stalk celery, chopped

3 cloves garlic, peeled and minced

¼ cup chopped fresh parsley

1 cup dry white wine, such as sauvignon blanc

1 (8-ounce) can tomato sauce

1 (28-ounce) can whole tomatoes, drained

Dash cayenne pepper

Salt and pepper to taste

½ teaspoon dried basil

1 bay leaf

2 pounds crab claws or frozen lobster tails, thawed

1 pound cod or red snapper, cut into chunks

½ pound fresh shrimp, shelled and deveined (you can leave the tails on if desired, to add more flavor)

1½ pound clams, cleaned (see our Tip)

8 large sea scallops (if very large, cut in half)

Crushed red pepper flakes, optional

1. Heat the oil in a large skillet over MEDIUM heat. Add the onion, celery, green pepper,

SERVES: 4 to 6
SLOW COOKER SIZE: 6 quart
PREP TIME: 15 minutes
COOKING TIME: 4½ to 6½ hours on LOW

Serving Suggestions

A good crusty French or sourdough bread is a must with this meal. The best part is mopping up the juices with the bread at the end. Because this is a light meal, you can go decadent for dessert, if desired. Did someone say cheesecake?

Variations

You can economize and use just one or two types of fish or shellfish in this dish. It won't be cioppino, but it will still be good.

Tip

Hard-shell clams should be tightly closed and unbroken when purchased. If the shell is open a little bit, tap the shell

garlic and parsely and sauté until soft, about 5 minutes. Place in the slow cooker.

2. Add the wine, tomato sauce, whole tomatoes, cayenne pepper, salt and pepper, dried basil, and bay leaf to slow cooker and stir with a wooden spoon to combine, breaking up the whole tomatoes into small pieces. Cover and cook on LOW for 4 to 6 hours.

3. Increase the heat to HIGH and add all the fish to the slow cooker. Cover and cook on HIGH for *30 minutes more* until all the clams have opened and all fish and shellfish are fully cooked.

4. Taste before serving. If necessary, reseason with a dash of salt, pepper, or red pepper flakes. Remove the bay leaf and serve hot in large soup bowls. You can pass extra crushed red pepper flakes around the table for those who want to add a pinch of "heat."

and if the clam is alive and safe to eat, it will snap shut. Before you cook clams make sure you scrub them under cold water to remove any dirt or grit.

To remove sand inside commercial, store-bought clams, rinse them thoroughly in cold running water or let them soak for *half an hour.* If you dig them yourself, soak them for a few hours in salted water to which you've added a handful of cornmeal. Be sure to change the water at least once. Drain and rinse again and the clams will be ready for cooking.

each Butter

When peaches come into season, this is a good way to cook them up so you can enjoy them all year long. A friend shared this recipe with us many years ago and it's been a favorite ever since. It's best to cook this in an out-of-the-way corner of the kitchen, or someplace in the house where things won't accidentally be dropped into the open pot.

4 pounds peaches, peeled, pitted, and quartered

Grated zest of 1 lemon

¼ cup fresh lemon juice

2 cups sugar

2 teaspoons ground cinnamon

½ teaspoon ground cloves

1. Place peaches, lemon zest, and lemon juice in slow cooker. Stir to coat peaches well with lemon juice. Cover and cook on HIGH for 4 hours until very soft.

2. Stir in the remaining ingredients, *do not cover,* and cook on HIGH 4 hours more, stirring occasionally. Mash by hand with a potato masher or purée with an immersion blender. When pureed, the butter should be quite thick—almost the consistency of jam. If not, continue cooking 1 to 2 more hours *uncovered* until it reaches the desired consistency. Ladle into freezer containers or sterilized jars.

YIELDS: about 3 pints

SLOW COOKER SIZE: 4 quart

PREP TIME: 30 minutes

COOKING TIME: 8–10 hours on HIGH

Serving Suggestions:

This is especially good spread on toasted whole wheat bread. For something different, grill a ham steak for dinner, and at the end brush both sides with some of this peach butter.

Variations

You could substitute other fruits such as pears, pineapple, or apricots for half of the peaches.

Tip

To peel peaches with ease, first dip them in a saucepan filled with simmering water for 20 to 30 seconds. Cool slightly under cold running water or dunk them in a large bowl of ice water, then slip the skins off with a knife.

$\mathcal{P}$icnic Beans

These beans would be a hit at any picnic or family gathering, but don't wait until then to to try them.

- ¹⁄₂ pound ground beef
- 1 medium onion, chopped
- 2 (16-ounce) cans Bush or B&M baked beans
- 1 (15-ounce) can kidney beans, drained and rinsed
- 1 (15-ounce) can lima beans, drained and rinsed
- ¹⁄₂ green pepper, stemmed, seeded and chopped
- 2 tablespoons dark brown sugar
- ¹⁄₄ cup unsulphured molasses
- ¹⁄₄ cup Dijon mustard
- 1 tablespoon Worcestershire sauce
- ¹⁄₄ teaspoon hot pepper sauce
- 1 teaspoon salt

1. In a nonstick skillet over MEDIUM HEAT, cook the ground beef and onion until meat is no longer pink. Drain and add to slow cooker.

2. Place rest of ingredients in slow cooker and stir to combine. Cover and cook on LOW for 4 to 8 hours.

SERVES: 6

SLOW COOKER SIZE: 4 quart

PREP TIME: 20 minutes

COOKING TIME: 4 to 8 hours on LOW

Serving Suggestions

Serve with barbequed beef brisket, grilled sausages, or just plain old hot dogs. Begin or end the meal with a fresh fruit salad or slices of watermelon.

Variations

You can vary the types of beans and use garbanzos, pinto beans, cannellini beans, even black-eyed peas, if you prefer. You could also substitute thinly sliced kielbasa for the ground beef—no need to brown it first.

Tip

Spray the measuring cup with cooking oil before measuring molasses or honey and it will slide out with ease.

*I*talian Beef Sandwiches

Slow-cooking turns an inexpensive, rather tough cut of meat into a delectable buffet dish for a crowd.

1 (3- to 4-pound) chuck, rump, top round, bottom
    round or eye of round roast

1 (14-ounce) can beef broth

1 tablespoon Worcestershire sauce

1 medium onion, peeled and sliced

2 cloves garlic, peeled and slivered

1 (1.3-ounce) package dry, Lipton's Beefy Onion
    Soup mix

2 tablespoons Italian seasoning

Pepper to taste

Sandwich buns or French rolls

1. Cut roast in half to fit in slow cooker, if necessary. Place all ingredients, except buns or rolls, in slow cooker. Cover and cook on LOW for 8 to 10 hours.

2. Remove beef and slice thinly across the grain. Serve on sandwich rolls with more salt and pepper if desired. Skim fat from juices and serve warm from the slow cooker for dunking or pouring over the beef.

SERVES: 8 to 10	
SLOW COOKER SIZE: 4 quart	
PREP TIME: 5 minutes	
COOKING TIME: 8 to10 hours on LOW	

Serving Suggestions

Serve with macaroni salad and sliced oranges.

Variations

You could easily make this into a chopped-beef sandwich instead: after slicing the beef, chop into very small pieces and return to juices in the pot. Serve warm.

Tip

Beef and chicken broths are now available in resealable cartons—great when you only need to use a little. Once opened, you can store them in the refrigerator up to 10 days.

*E*asy Overnight BBQ Beef or Pork Sandwiches

This standby comes in handy when we can't think of what to serve a hungry crowd at tailgate parties or camp-outs. It's great to have in your repertoire when time is at a premium. This cooks overnight while you sleep.

1 (2½- to 3-pound) chuck roast or brisket, trimmed of all fat and cut in half crosswise, 2 or 1 (2½- to 3-pound) boneless pork shoulder or Boston butt roast (or 4-pound roast, bone in), trimmed of all fat and cut in half crosswise

1 (18- to 20-ounce) bottle of your favorite barbeque sauce

Hamburger buns or sandwich rolls

1. Late at night before going to bed, place meat in slow cooker and pour the sauce on top. Cover and cook on LOW for 8 to 10 hours.

2. The next morning, remove and discard any bones and remaining fat. Allow mixture to cool, then shred meat in the pot using two forks. Place in plastic zip-top bags and refrigerate until needed.

3. About 2 hours before serving, return mixture to a washed and dried slow cooker and reheat on HIGH. Serve straight from the slow cooker on toasted buns.

SERVES: 8
SLOW COOKER SIZE: 4 quart
PREP TIME: 5 minutes
COOKING TIME: 8 to 10 hours on LOW

Serving Suggestions

Serve baked beans, corn on the cob, pickles, and coleslaw. Homemade brownies with a handful of chocolate chips thrown in the batter make a wonderful dessert.

Variations

For maximum flavor, first brown the meat in 2 tablespoons oil. We've tried this using two pork tenderloins with great results.

You can also cook this in one day by starting it first thing in the morning.

Tip

Freeze in single serving sizes in zip-top bags for quick heat-and-eat sandwiches later on.

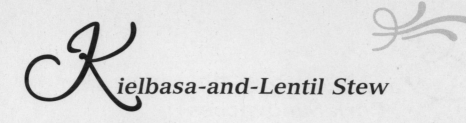

Kielbasa-and-Lentil Stew

The kielbasa gives this stew its flavor, the cayenne a touch of heat, and the lentils add a wholesome touch. It's a tasty way to add legumes to your diet.

2 cups water

2 teaspoons beef bouillon base or 2 bouillon cubes

1½ cups lentils, rinsed

1 pound kielbasa sliced ¼-inch thick

2 stalks celery, sliced ¼-inch thick

1 medium onion, peeled and finely chopped

1 clove garlic, minced

1 (16-ounce) can diced tomatoes, undrained

½ teaspoon Italian seasoning

¼ teaspoon cayenne pepper

1. Place all ingredients in slow cooker and stir to combine. Cover and cook on LOW for 6 to 8 hours.

2. Taste before serving. If necessary, reseason with a dash of salt, pepper, and any other flavors that may have cooked out.

SERVES: 6

SLOW COOKER SIZE: 4 quart

PREP TIME: 15 minutes

COOKING TIME: 6 to 8 hours on LOW

Serving Suggestions

Serve with sliced apples for starters, then some steamed banana squash on the side. If you have children, they'd get a kick out of microwaved s'mores for dessert. Simply place a square of a milk chocolate candy bar or a sprinkle of chocolate chips on a graham cracker square. Place a large marshmallow on top, then top with another graham cracker. Microwave on HIGH 10 to 15 seconds.

Variations

To lighten, substitute turkey kielbasa for the regular kielbasa.

Tip

Here's a "magical" way to rid your hands of the smell of garlic. Grab a stainless steel pot or utensil and then run tap water over your hands. Gone!

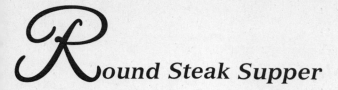ound Steak Supper

Linda's mother-in-law Bernadette used to make this dish when they flew home to Chicago to visit. It was quick and easy and gave them all more time to sit around the kitchen table playing pinochle for hours on end. She cooked it on the stovetop, but it easliy converts to the slow cooker.

1 (3-pound) top or bottom round steak, trimmed of fat and cut into 6 serving pieces

1 (12-ounce) bottle chili sauce

12 stalks celery, sliced

Salt and pepper to taste

1. Place all ingredients in slow cooker in order listed. Cover and cook on LOW for 8 to 10 hours.

2. Taste before serving. If necessary, reseason with a dash of salt and pepper.

SERVES: 6

SLOW COOKER SIZE: 4 quart

PREP TIME: 10 minutes

COOKING TIME: 8 to 10 hours on LOW

Serving Suggestions

Boiled potatoes and steamed green beans complete this dish. And, as Bernadette often did, serve sliced angel food cake topped with a large dollop of lemon pudding for dessert.

Variations

To bring out more of the beef flavor, you could brown the round steak first in a little vegetable oil. To save time, after 4 hours add several potatoes to the slow cooker rather than boiling them and serving separately.

ips

To revitalize limp celery stalks, place them in some ice water in the refrigerator for several hours.

If using very large stalks of celery, slice them in half lengthwise first before slicing crosswise.

$\mathcal{V}$egetable Chili

Linda has had this recipe in her files for twenty years. It has stood the test of time and is as good today as it was back in the '80s. We changed a few ingredients and adapted it for the slow cooker. Voilà—a hearty, healthy chili for the new millennium.

1 tablespoon olive oil

2 large onions, peeled and finely chopped

4 cups peeled and diced eggplant, cut into ½-inch cubes

2 cloves garlic, minced

3 large carrots, peeled and cut into ½-inch cubes

2 large green peppers, seeded and chopped

3 large stalks celery, chopped

1 jalapeño pepper, minced

1 (14.5-ounce) can diced tomatoes, undrained

2 tablespoons tomato paste

1 teaspoon sugar

2 tablespoons chili powder

2 teaspoons ground cumin

¼ teaspoon red pepper flakes, or to taste

¼ cup dry red wine

½ cup vegetable broth or 1 cube vegetable bouillon and ½ cup water

Salt and pepper to taste

1 (15-ounce) can red kidney beans, rinsed and drained

1 (15-ounce) can garbanzo beans, rinsed and drained

GARNISHES:

chopped onion

sour cream

SERVES: 8

SLOW COOKER SIZE: 4 quart

PREP TIME: 35 minutes

COOKING TIME: 4 to 6 hours on LOW

Serving Suggestions

This chili is great served over hot rice, warm couscous, or cooked spaghetti.

Variations

You can subsitute chopped zucchini for the eggplant.

You can omit the wine and substitute vegetable broth.

Tip

Look for tomato paste in tubes. What you don't use can be kept in the refrigerator for next time, instead of tossed out.

fresh cilantro

cubes of fresh avocado

grated cheddar or Monterey jack cheese

1. Place all ingredients, except the beans and garnishes, in slow cooker and stir to combine.

2. Cover and cook on LOW for 4 to 6 hours. Stir in the beans and cook 30 minutes more.

3. Taste before serving. If necessary, reseason with a dash of salt, pepper, and any other flavors that may have cooked out. Serve warm and garnish as desired.

Slow-Cooked Jambalaya

This dish is worthy of Grandma's antique soup tureen, or can be served straight from the slow cooker. Don't forget to pass around the bottle of hot pepper sauce!

1 onion, peeled and chopped

3 cloves garlic, peeled and minced

1 pound boneless, skinless chicken breasts or tenders, cut into bite-size pieces.

1 green bell pepper, stemmed, seeded and chopped

2 large stalks celery, sliced

1 to 2 jalapeño peppers, thinly sliced

1 (14¹/₂-ounce) can diced tomatoes, with juice

1 (6-ounce) can tomato paste

1 teaspoon hot pepper sauce

1 teaspoon salt

¹/₂ teaspoon pepper

1 pound medium shrimp, shelled, halved lengthwise and deveined

¹/₂ pound kielbasa or Polish sausage, halved lengthwise and sliced 1 inch thick

3 tablespoons chopped fresh parsley

1 tablespoon chopped fresh oregano

1 tablespoon fresh thyme leaves

4 cups cooked rice

1. Place the first 11 ingredients in slow cooker and stir to combine. Cover and cook on LOW for 6 to 8 hours.

SERVES: 6
SLOW COOKER SIZE: 4 quart
PREP TIME: 30 minutes
COOKING TIME: 6 to 8 hours on LOW

Serving Suggestions

Serve with frosty glasses of beer or lemonade, and bring out strawberry shortcake for dessert.

Variations

You can vary the taste by using leftover turkey in place of the chicken, or even a firm white fish such as cod. The fish would need to be added the last 30 minutes.

Tip

Don't throw away those shrimp shells! Place them in a bag in your freezer for shrimp stock. When needed, place shells in small saucepan and cover with about 6 cups water. Simmer on MEDIUM-LOW for 1 to 2 hours. Strain through fine sieve.

2. Turn heat to HIGH. Stir in the shrimp, sausage, parsley, oregano, and thyme, and cook another 30 minutes until the shrimp is fully cooked.

3. Taste before serving. If necessary, reseason with a dash of salt, pepper, and any other flavors that may have cooked out. Serve hot over rice in large soup bowls.

Tamera's Pot Roast and Potatoes

This recipe was given to Linda by one of the sweetest middle school teachers ever, Tamera Surovchak. Her mom Betty Hamm created this recipe. It's a good one when you need an easy, comforting meal—whether it's midwinter or the height of summer!

2- to 3-pound beef pot roast, trimmed of fat

2 tablespoons A-1 Steak Sauce

1 (1-ounce) package dry onion soup mix

2 (10-ounce) cans cream of mushroom soup

2 cloves garlic, peeled and minced

Salt and pepper to taste

1 (8-ounce) package fresh mushrooms, trimmed and wiped clean with damp cloth

20 to 30 baby white potatoes, 1½ to 2 pounds, scrubbed

1. Place roast in slow cooker and generously coat it with steak sauce on all sides. Sprinkle dry onion soup mix on top then pour mushroom soup on top. Sprinkle garlic over soup and add salt and pepper to taste. Top with mushrooms and potatoes. Cover and cook on LOW for 6 to 8 hours.

2. Taste before serving. If necessary, reseason with a dash of salt and pepper.

SERVES: 4 to 6

SLOW COOKER SIZE: 4½ quart

PREP TIME: 15 minutes

COOKING TIME: 6 to 8 hours on LOW

Serving Suggestions

To round out this one-pot meal, serve a tossed green salad and some snow peas quickly sautéed in a drizzle of sesame oil. For an easy dessert, split a store-bought brownie in half horizontally and spread some marshmallow cream on the bottom half. Replace the top half and serve. Yum!

Variations

This recipe makes quite a bit of gravy. To lighten it, omit one can of soup and use fewer potatoes.

Tip

Mushrooms are very porous and will absorb a great deal of water if you drown them in water to clean them. Instead, use a damp cloth and just brush off any dirt.

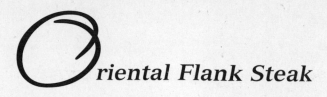riental Flank Steak

Don't attempt this one if you're going to be gone all day: it only takes 4 to 5 hours to cook. It's a savior if you have company coming with just a few hours' notice.

¹/₄ cup rice wine or dry sherry

¹/₄ cup soy sauce

2 tablespoons Worcestershire sauce

1 clove garlic, peeled and minced

¹/₈ to ¹/₄ teaspoon crushed red pepper flakes, to taste

1 tablespoon minced fresh ginger

Salt and pepper to taste

1 (1¹/₂- to 2-pound) flank steak, trimmed of fat and cut to fit slow cooker

1. Place all ingredients, except steak, in slow cooker and stir to combine. Add steak, spoon sauce over, cover, and cook on LOW for 4 to 5 hours.

2. Taste before serving. If necessary, reseason with a dash of salt and pepper.

3. Remove steak, allow to rest for 5 to 10 minutes, then slice across the grain in very thin slices.

SERVES: 4
SLOW COOKER SIZE: 4 quart
PREP TIME: 10 minutes
COOKING TIME: 4 to 5 hours on LOW

Serving Suggestions

Start with a salad of sliced cucumber and onion tossed in a dressing of 2 tablespoons oil and 2 teaspoons seasoned rice vinegar. For an easy side dish, briefly stir-fry some sliced red bell pepper, onion, and fresh snow peas in a little peanut oil and serve over cooked rice.

Variations

You could substitute a pork tenderloin—but if you do, reduce the cooking time to 2 hours.

Tip

When stir-frying vegetables, it's best to use peanut or vegetable oil. They have a higher smoking point than other oils and won't ignite as easily over high heat.

sso Buco

If this seems a little exotic to you, try it once and you may find this company meal will become a specialty of the house. With this dish in front of you and Pavarotti on the stereo, you'll be transported to the shores of sunny Italy! And don't overlook the marrow; some people consider it the best part of the dish. You can scoop it out with a chop stick or iced tea spoon.

4 veal shanks, about 2 inches thick

Kitchen twine

Flour for dredging

Salt and pepper to taste

2 tablespoons butter

2 tablespoons olive oil

1 small onion, peeled and finely chopped

1 carrot, peeled, finely chopped

1 stalk celery, finely chopped

1 clove garlic, peeled and minced

1 (14-ounce) can beef or chicken broth

¹/₂ cup dry white wine

2 tablespoons tomato paste

A bouquet garni* of 4 sprigs of fresh parsley,
1 sprig of rosemary, 1 sprig of fresh thyme, and
1 bay leaf

Salt and pepper to taste

GARNISHES:

1 tablespoon grated lemon zest

¹/₄ cup flat-leaf parsley, finely chopped

1. Tie a piece of twine around each veal shank (the short way) to keep the meat from falling off the bone during cooking.

SERVES: 4

SLOW COOKER SIZE: 4 quart

PREP TIME: 50 minutes

COOKING TIME: 5 to 6 hours on LOW

Serving Suggestions

These are wonderful served over garlic mashed potatoes or with a creamy lemon risotto. Bunches of fresh spinach sautéed in olive oil and minced garlic would complete the picture. We doubt there will be any room left for dessert after this hearty meal!

Variations

Veal shanks can be hard to find, but lamb shanks will also work in this recipe.

Tip

*To create a bouquet garni, spread a 9-inch-square piece of cheesecloth on the counter and fill with the fresh herbs. Bring all four corners to the center and tie securely with a piece of

2. Pat veal shanks dry with paper towels. Season the flour with salt and pepper then dredge veal shanks in flour mixture. Set aside.

3. In a deep skillet or large Dutch oven, heat the butter and oil over MEDIUM-HIGH heat until it melts. Add the veal shanks and brown well on both sides, about 8 minutes total. Remove and place in slow cooker.

4. Reduce the heat to MEDIUM and add the chopped onion, carrot, and celery to the pan. Sauté until the onion is soft, about 3 minutes. Add the garlic and cook 1 minute more.

5. Stir in the wine, broth, and tomato paste; bring to a boil, scraping up browned bits from the bottom of the pan. Boil and stir until the liquid is reduced by half, about 4 minutes.

6. Pour the sauce over the veal shanks in the slow cooker. Bury the bouquet garni in the sauce. Cover and cook on LOW for 5 to 6 hours.

7. To serve, remove the twine from the veal shanks and place them on a serving dish. Remove the bouquet garni and discard. Season the sauce to taste with salt and pepper, then pour over the shanks. Combine the chopped parsley and lemon zest and sprinkle on top.

kitchen twine, leaving long strands for easy removal from the slow cooker.

Orange-Glazed Pork Chops

These tasty pork chops cook in a syrupy orange sauce that could be served in a gravy boat as a topping for the rice, noodles, or potatoes you serve as a side dish.

2 tablespoons oil

6 pork loin chops, 1 inch thick, trimmed of fat

3 tablespoon minced onion

2 cups orange juice

¼ cup orange marmalade

¼ cup light brown sugar

1½ teaspoons dry mustard

1 teaspoon salt

SERVES: 6
SLOW COOKER SIZE: 4 quart
PREP TIME: 25 minutes
COOKING TIME: 3 to 4 hours on LOW

1. Heat the oil in a large skillet over medium heat. Add the pork chops and brown both sides, about 5 minutes per side.

2. Transfer the chops to the slow cooker.

3. Pour off all but 1 tablespoon of oil from the skillet. Return to the heat and add the onion. Cook for 1 minute.

4. Turn the heat up to medium-high and add the orange juice, marmalade, brown sugar, dry mustard, and salt, whisking to blend. Bring to a full boil, stirring frequently. Boil and stir for 6 minutes until the sauce has a thin syrupy consistency, scraping up any brown bits from the bottom of the pan.

Serving Suggestions

Serve these over rice with some of the sauce drizzled on top. Steamed carrots sliced on a diagonal, sliced onion, and fresh or frozen Chinese snow peas, quickly stir-fried in a little oil, would make a healthy, colorful side dish. For dessert, drop a little fresh fruit in some large ice cream cones and top with a double scoop of your favorite frozen yogurt.

Variations

To save time (but lose flavor), skip step 1 and just place pork chops in slow cooker without browning first.

Tip

Be careful when pouring the hot syrupy sauce into the crockery pot. It's best to place the pot in the sink and pour the sauce into

5. Pour the sauce over the pork chops in the cooker, rotating them with tongs to completely coat both sides with the sauce.

6. Cover and cook on LOW for 3 to 4 hours until tender to the touch.

it there. If you accidently spill, you won't burn yourself or have a mess to clean up.

$\mathcal{D}$ebbie's Lamb Curry and Rice

Linda's sister Debbie makes a wonderful lamb curry and rice with leftover lamb. Linda and Debbie came up with this slow cooker version, a close facsimile of the original.

3 tablespoons olive oil

2 pounds boneless leg of lamb or lamb shoulder,
   cut in 1-inch pieces

2 tablespoons butter

1 onion, sliced

½ cup flour

Salt and pepper to taste

4 teaspoons curry powder or to taste

½ teaspoon ground cumin

1 (14-ounce) can chicken broth

1½ cups water

1 cup heavy cream

Cooked rice

OPTIONAL CONDIMENTS:

chopped peanuts

chopped hard boiled eggs

golden raisins

chutney

1. Heat the oil in a large skillet over MEDIUM-HIGH heat. Add the lamb and cook until brown, 15 to 20 minutes turning once. Remove with slotted spoon and place in slow cooker.

2. Reduce heat to MEDIUM and add butter to skillet. When melted, sauté the onion until soft,

---

SERVES: 4

SLOW COOKER SIZE: 4 quart

PREP TIME: 40 minutes

COOKING TIME: 6 to 8 hours on LOW

Serving Suggestions

A cooling lime gelatin salad would go well with this spicy dish. Serve steamed carrots and peas for a side dish.

Variations

You could add a couple of sliced carrots and even some canned garbanzo beans to this simple dish to back it up.

Tip

Buy a 4-pound boneless leg of lamb and have the butcher cut it in half. Roast or grill one half and freeze the other half to use in this dish at a later date. If you love curry dishes, take time to find a good Madras (Indian) curry powder in a gourmet market or online.

about 5 minutes. Stir in flour, salt, pepper, 2 teaspoons curry powder, and cumin. Heat through.

3. Stir in chicken broth and water, stirring constantly and scraping up browned bits, until the mixture comes to a boil and thickens.

4. Pour gravy over lamb in slow cooker and stir to combine. Cover and cook on LOW for 6 to 8 hours.

5. About 20 minutes before serving, stir in the cream and the remaining 2 teaspoons curry powder and heat through.

6. Taste before serving. If necessary, reseason with a dash of salt, pepper, and additional curry. Serve over rice with condiments of choice.

$\mathcal{P}$olynesian Chicken

If your pantry or freezer are well stocked, you could throw this together in a flash without a trip to the market.

3½ pounds boneless, skinless chicken breasts

Salt and pepper to taste

1 cup barbeque sauce

2 tablespoons peach preserves

2 tablespoons soy sauce

½ cup chopped onion

1 (8-ounce) can sliced water chestnuts, drained

1 large green bell pepper, seeds removed and
   chopped

1. Place chicken in bottom of slow cooker and sprinkle with salt and pepper.

2. In a bowl, combine the barbeque sauce, peach preserves, soy sauce, and onion. Pour over the chicken.

3. Cover and cook on LOW for 5 to 6 hours. Add the water chestnuts and green pepper and cook 30 minutes more.

SERVES: 6

SLOW COOKER SIZE: 4 quart

PREP TIME: 10 minutes

COOKING TIME: 6 to 8 hours on LOW

Serving Suggestions

Serve this with cooked rice and a good three-bean salad.

Serve fresh, sliced plums for dessert.

Variations

You could substitute a red bell pepper for the green. If you have some Peach Butter handy (see page 100), you could substitute it for the peach preserves.

Tip

There are several types of soy sauce. If you're concerned about sodium, try a light soy sauce labeled.

*L*emon-Lime Chicken
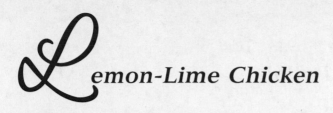

What a good way to get your vitamin C! The citrus adds such a sunny flavor to this simple chicken dish.

¹/₄ cup butter or margarine, melted

¹/₄ cup fresh lemon juice

¹/₄ cup fresh lime juice

¹/₂ teaspoon turmeric

2 cloves garlic, peeled and minced

¹/₂ teaspoon salt

¹/₄ teaspoon pepper

1 (3- to 3¹/₂-pound) whole chicken, or chicken pieces

1. Place all ingredients, except chicken, in slow cooker and stir to combine. Add chicken and coat well with sauce. Cover and cook on LOW for 6 to 8 hours.

2. Taste before serving. If necessary, reseason with a dash of salt, pepper, and any other flavors that may have been diluted during cooking.

SERVES: 4

SLOW COOKER SIZE: 4 quart

PREP TIME: 10 minutes

COOKING TIME: 6 to 8 hours on LOW

Serving Suggestions

You could serve this with wild rice and grilled asparagus. Peel thick stalks of asparagus with vegetable peeler, marinate in a little bottled balsamic vinaigrette dressing, then place on the grill or under the broiler for several minutes until browned and tender. Dress with toasted sesame seeds or sliced almonds.

Variations

We like to turn this into Lemon-Lime-Rosemary Chicken by substituting 1 tablespoon minced fresh rosemary for the turmeric.

Tip

If you choose to make this the night before, so it will be ready to take out of the refrigerator and put in your slow cooker, combine the sauce ingredients in the pot, but do not add the raw chicken until the morning.

iva el Pollo!

Step back into the '60s with this retro chicken casserole. Linda remembers when they were newlyweds this was the dish to serve when company was coming. Long gone are the harvest gold appliances, the avocado green shag carpeting and the heavy, dark Mediterranean furniture with the orange cushions. Thank goodness! But if you ever have a hankering for a taste of days past, here's the dish to try.

1 tablespoon butter or cooking oil spray

1 ($10^3/_4$-ounce) can condensed cream of mushroom soup

1 ($10^3/_4$-ounce) can condensed cream of chicken soup

$1/_2$ cup finely grated onion

1 cup (8 ounces) salsa verde (green chili sauce)

1 cup sour cream

12 corn tortillas, each cut into 8 strips

4 cups (about 2 pounds) diced, cooked chicken

$1^1/_2$ cups (6 ounces) grated cheddar cheese

1. Butter or spray the bottom and sides of the slow cooker pot.

2. In a medium bowl, combine the soups, onion, salsa, and sour cream. Set aside.

3. Place $1/_3$ of the tortilla stips on the bottom of the pot. Scatter $1/_3$ of the cooked chicken on top, then spread $1/_3$ of the soup mixture evenly over the chicken. Repeat the layers

---

SERVES: 6

SLOW COOKER SIZE: 4 quart

PREP TIME: 30 minutes

COOKING TIME: 5 to 6 hours on LOW

Serving Suggestions

Serve with a relish tray of raw veggies and fresh fruit kabobs for dessert.

Variations

Try mixing and matching different soups, such as cream of celery, tomato, etc.

Tip

For the cooked chicken, use boneless, skinless chicken breasts or chicken tenders. Place them in a large saucepan, cover with water, and bring just to a boil. Turn off the heat, cover, and let sit for 30 minutes to finish cooking. Time saving tip: as long as you're cooking chicken for this recipe, double

two more times, ending with the soup mixture.

4. Cover and cook on LOW for 5 to 6 hours.

5. Sprinkle with cheese and serve.

the amount, then freeze the
other half for use at another
time.

$\mathcal{B}$eef-and-Pasta Pot

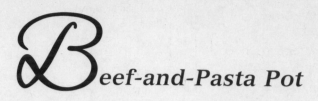

This could easily become a standard in your household. It's quick, easy, and fun to think of variations for. Try it and see!

1 pound ground beef

1 onion, chopped

1 cup water

1 (12-ounce) can tomato paste

1/3 cup dry red wine or water

1 teaspoon beef bouillon base or 1 beef bouillon cube

1 teaspoon Italian seasoning

1 teaspoon sugar

1 pound penne pasta, cooked al dente

2 cups grated mozzarella cheese

1. In a nonstick skillet, brown the ground beef and onions over medium heat, about 5 minutes. Drain and pour into the slow cooker pot.

2. Add the water, tomato paste, wine, beef base, Italian seasoning, and sugar to the slow cooker; stir to combine.

3. Cover and cook on LOW for 6 to 8 hours.

4. Stir in the cooked penne and cheese and serve. Adding a little of the pasta cooking water will thin the sauce, if desired.

SERVES: 4
SLOW COOKER SIZE: 4 quart
PREP TIME: 15 minutes
COOKING TIME: 6 to 8 hours on LOW

Serving Suggestions

Begin the meal with an antipasto platter of bite-size morsels, such as marinated artichoke hearts, pepperoncini peppers, olives, miniature balls of mozzarella cheese, thinly sliced salami or pepperoni, marinated, grilled veggies, or cherry tomatoes.

Add a basket of warm garlic bread or bread sticks.

Variations

To lighten this recipe, substitute ground turkey or turkey sausage for the beef, and omit the cheese or use reduced fat cheese.

Tip

Cook the pasta al dente, which means "to the tooth" in Italian. The pasta should still have some body to it and not be mushy.

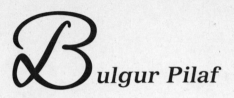ulgur Pilaf

This is a lovely side dish, when you crave something earthy to take the place of rice.

2 cups bulgur wheat

8 ounces button mushrooms (about 13 to 14), cleaned and cut in half

4 carrots or 2 small zucchini, shredded

1 large onion, peeled and chopped

1 clove garlic, peeled and minced

2 (14-ounce) cans beef or vegetable broth

2 tablespoons butter or margarine, cut into small pieces

1 tablespoon fresh thyme or 1 teaspoon dried

1 teaspoon salt

1 teaspoon ground cumin

¼ teaspoon ground cayenne pepper

1. Place all ingredients in slow cooker and stir to combine. Cover and cook on LOW for 3 to 4 hours.

2. Taste before serving. If necessary, reseason.

SERVES: 4	
SLOW COOKER SIZE: 4 quart	
PREP TIME: 10 minutes	
COOKING TIME: 3 to 4 hours on LOW	

Serving Suggestions

Serve with smoked turkey, sliced green and red bell peppers, and onion, sautéed til tender in a little oil. Finish with sliced apples and a fat-free caramel-apple dip.

Variations

Try adding more veggies to create a vegetarian meal in one pot, such as chopped broccoli, green bell peppers, diced chilies, asparagus, or diced butternut squash and some shredded cheese.

Tip

To keep the oils in bulgur from turning rancid over time, store it in the freezer.

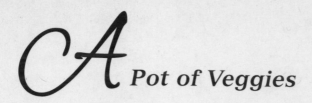 Pot of Veggies

Try this vegetarian alternative to turning on the oven or grill when the thermometer outside nears triple digits.

6 small red potatoes, quartered

2 large carrots, peeled and cut into small chunks

1 large onion, peeled and quartered

2 large cloves garlic, chopped

$\frac{1}{2}$ green pepper, cut into strips

$\frac{1}{2}$ red, orange, or yellow pepper, cut into strips

$\frac{1}{2}$ small head of cabbage, cut into chunks

1 fennel bulb, trimmed, stalks removed, and cut into thick slices

2 tablespoons olive oil

Salt and pepper to taste

1. Place all vegetables in slow cooker. Drizzle oil over them and stir well to coat. (Initially the vegetables will fill the pot almost to the brim, so stir in the olive oil carefully, or combine them in a separate bowl first. As they cook, the vegetables will reduce significantly.)

2. Cover and cook on LOW heat for 4 to 6 hours.

3. Taste before serving. If necessary, reseason with a dash of salt and pepper.

SERVES: 4

SLOW COOKER SIZE: 4 quart

PREP TIME: 10 minutes

COOKING TIME: 4 to 6 hours on LOW

Serving Suggestions

Serve with grilled pork chops and homemade applesauce.

Variations

To add more flavor, during the last half hour of cooking stir in freshly grated ginger, the zest of 1 lemon or $\frac{1}{2}$ orange, a dash or two of red pepper flakes, or a small handful of chopped fresh herbs, such as rosemary, thyme, oregano, or dill.

You can vary the vegetables to match what you might have in your refrigerator.

Tip

You can cut back on salt, if you squeeze a little lemon juice on the vegetables instead.

Garlic Potato Chunks
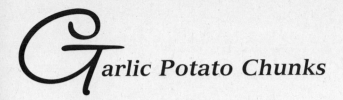

In the summertime, throw a steak on the grill, cook up these potatoes in the slow cooker, and you'll never have to heat up the kitchen. That's a good thing!

6 medium russet potatoes, well scrubbed and cut
   into 1-inch chunks

1 medium onion, peeled and coarsely chopped

3 cloves garlic, chopped

1 tablespoon olive oil

Salt and pepper to taste

1. Place all ingredients in slow cooker and stir to combine. Cover and cook on LOW for 6 to 8 hours.

2. Taste before serving. If necessary, reseason with a dash of salt and pepper.

SERVES: 6

SLOW COOKER SIZE: 4 quart

PREP TIME: 15 minutes

COOKING TIME: 6 to 8 hours on LOW

Serving Suggestions

To avoid turning on the stove, just serve a lush green salad with our suggested grilled steak and these potatoes. Some lemon sorbet for dessert sounds perfect.

Variations

The seasonings you can add to this dish are limited only by your imagination. Try fresh rosemary, parsley, chives, grated citrus rind, curry powder, or Cajun seasoning.

Tip

If adding fresh herbs, stir them in during the last 15 minutes so they won't loose their potency.

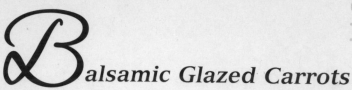

Balsamic Glazed Carrots

Most grocery stores carry bags of ready-to-use baby carrots in the produce section—they make this side dish a cinch to prepare.

1 2-pound bag of baby carrots

Salt and pepper to taste

¼ cup balsamic vinegar

2 tablespoons honey

2 tablespoons dark brown sugar

2 tablespoon butter

1. Place carrots in slow cooker and season with salt and pepper.

2. In a small saucepan over medium-high heat, bring the vinegar to a boil. Boil 4 to 5 minutes until reduced by half. Remove from heat.

3. Add honey, sugar, and butter to vinegar reduction and stir until the butter melts. Pour over carrots, cover, and cook on LOW for 4 to 6 hours.

4. Taste before serving. If necessary, reseason.

SERVES: 6	
SLOW COOKER SIZE: 4 quart	
PREP TIME: 10 minutes	
COOKING TIME: 4 to 6 hours on LOW	

Serving Suggestions

Serve with grilled steaks, baked potatoes, and packets of grilled sweet onions such as Vidalias. To prepare the onions, thinly slice one onion for every two or three people you're serving. Tear off a square of heavy-duty foil (or 2 squares of regular foil). Place a pat of butter on the foil, add the onions, another pat of butter on top, then salt and pepper to taste. Roll up all three edges to seal well. Place on a hot grill and cook about 10 minutes per side until the onions are nicely browned.

Variations

You can substitute 2 pounds regular size carrots for the baby carrots. Simply peel and cut into 1-inch chunks.

The longer balsamic vinegar is aged, the thicker and sweeter it becomes. The most expensive vinegars have been aged for decades in wooden casks, and are more like syrup, so should be used sparingly.

$\mathcal{U}$pside-down Peach Cobbler

The peaches start on the top and sink to the bottom during cooking. Try this very easy summer dessert soon.

1 tablespoon butter or cooking oil spray

2 cups Bisquick

1 cup sugar

½ teaspoon ground cinnamon

¼ cup butter or margarine, melted

1 cup milk

1 teaspoon vanilla

5 cups sliced peaches (about 5 large), peeled
   (see Tip)

½ cup sugar

¼ teaspoon ground cinnamon

⅛ teaspoon almond extract

Vanilla ice cream, frozen yogurt, or whipped cream

SERVES: 6

SLOW COOKER SIZE: 4 quart

PREP TIME: 20 minutes

COOKING TIME: 3 to 4 hours on HIGH

Serving Suggestions

Best served warm with ice cream or whipped cream.

Variations

Vary the fruit as desired. Substitute apples, berries, or a rhubarb-strawberry combination.

Tip

The easiest way to peel fresh peaches is to place them in a pot of simmering hot water for 20 to 30 seconds. Remove, run under cold water then slip the skins off with a sharp knife.

1. Butter or spray the bottom and sides of the slow cooker pot.

2. In a bowl, whisk together the Bisquick, 1 cup sugar, ½ teaspoon ground cinnamon, melted butter, milk, and vanilla until smooth. Pour into the bottom of the slow cooker.

3. In a bowl, combine the peaches, ½ cup sugar, ¼ teaspoon cinnamon, and almond extract. Pour on top of cake batter in slow cooker. Do not stir.

4. Cover and cook on HIGH for 3 to 4 hours, until the cake is set and fully cooked in the center. Turn off slow cooker, cool slightly for 15 minutes then serve in bowls topped with whipped cream or ice cream.

*P*iña Colada Bread Pudding with Rum Sauce

This luscious dessert will brighten up even the most mundane meal!

PUDDING:

1 tablespoon butter or cooking oil spray

1 (1-pound) loaf French bread, 2 or 3 days old, torn into bite-size pieces (about 12 cups)

1 large banana, sliced

1 tablespoon lemon juice

1 cup toasted sliced almonds

1 (8-ounce) can pineapple chunks with their juice

1 cup shredded, sweetened coconut

3 (12-ounce) cans evaporated milk

$\frac{1}{2}$ cup cream of coconut (see Tip)

$\frac{1}{2}$ cup sugar

3 eggs

3 tablespoons butter, melted

1 tablespoon vanilla extract

RUM SAUCE:

$\frac{3}{4}$ cup (1$\frac{1}{2}$ sticks) butter

1 cup powdered sugar

2 tablespoons dark rum or $\frac{1}{2}$ teaspoon rum flavoring

1. Butter or spray the bottom and sides of the slow cooker pot.

2. Place bread in slow cooker. In a small bowl, toss the sliced banana with lemon juice. Add

---

SERVES: 8

SLOW COOKER SIZE: 4$\frac{1}{2}$ quart

PREP TIME: 20 minutes

COOKING TIME: 5 to 7 hours on LOW

Serving Suggestions

We like serving this after a dinner of pork tenderloin and roasted green beans.

Variations

Try macadamia nuts instead of almonds for an authentic Hawaiian flavor.

Tip

Cream of coconut is a thick, sweetened coconut milk that can be found in either the canned milk section of your market or in the liquor department. Do not substitute plain coconut milk.

to slow cooker, along with the almonds, pineapple, and coconut. Stir to combine.

3. In a bowl, whisk together the milk, cream of coconut, sugar, eggs, butter, and vanilla extract. Pour over bread mixture. Cover and cook on LOW for 5 to 7 hours. Serve warm topped with rum sauce.

4. To make the sauce: in a saucepan over LOW heat, melt the butter. Slowly add the sugar, whisking constantly until the sugar dissolves. Stir in rum.

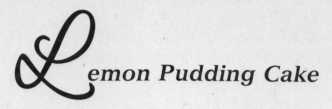emon Pudding Cake

Where's the lemon pudding? On the bottom!

4 eggs, separated

¹/₃ cup lemon juice (about 2 medium lemons)

1 tablespoon grated lemon zest

3 tablespoons butter, softened

1 cup all purpose flour

1 cup sugar

¹/₄ teaspoon salt

1¹/₂ cups milk

1. In a bowl, beat egg yolks, lemon juice, zest, and butter with an electric mixer about 2 minutes. Combine flour, sugar and salt; add to the yolk mixture alternately with the milk, beating well after each addition.

2. In a separate bowl, beat egg whites with electric mixer until stiff peaks form. Carefully fold into egg yolk mixture.

3. Pour mixture into slow cooker. Cover and cook on LOW 2 to 2¹/₂ hours, until cake is set on top.

SERVES: 6

SLOW COOKER SIZE: 4 quart

PREP TIME: 30 minutes

COOKING TIME: 2 to 2¹/₂ hours on HIGH

Serving Suggestions

This dessert would go well with a rich or spicy meal. You could serve it in parfait glasses with a dollop of whipped cream and a maraschino cherry on top.

Variations

You can lighten this dessert a little by using 1% milk instead of whole milk.

Tip

When separating eggs, break them over a small bowl first, then add them one by one to the mixing bowls. You want to avoid any yolk getting into the large bowl of egg whites and spoiling the whole batch. The fat from the yolk—or any other trace of grease or oil—will prevent the whites from forming properly.

resh Plum Delight

Lois's friend Lynn Head gave us the basics for this recipe. It's become one of our favorite summertime desserts!

6 tablespoons melted butter or margarine

4 cups (about 5) pitted and chopped fresh, ripe plums

2 tablespoons cornstarch

½ cup sugar

Heaping ¼ cup finely chopped crystalized ginger

1 (18.25-ounce) box white cake mix

Vanilla ice cream or frozen yogurt

1. Brush the bottom and sides of slow cooker pot with a little of the melted margarine

2. Place plums in slow cooker and sprinkle cornstarch on top. Gently toss together.

3. Sprinkle ginger and sugar evenly on top. Top with dry cake mix and drizzle melted butter over all.

4. Cover and cook on LOW for 6 to 8 hours. Serve warm with ice cream or frozen yogurt.

SERVES: 6

SLOW COOKER SIZE: 4 quart

PREP TIME: 15 minutes

COOKING TIME: 6 to 8 hours on LOW

Serving Suggestions

This delightful plum dessert is particularly well suited to accompany barbeque.

Variations

You can vary this recipe by substituting summer fruits, such as apricots or nectarines.

Tip

Choose plums that are ripe and ready to eat. Underripe plums have no flavor and overly ripe ones will not hold up well to cooking.

Autumn

Autumn

Glühwein

Caponata

Spinach Dip Ahoy!

Maria's Tortilla

Slow-Cooked Oatmeal

Beef-Bean-and-Barley Soup

Cream of Cauliflower Soup

Gulashsuppe

Dockside Chowder

Hot Beef Borscht

Slow Cooker Fondue

Granny's Apple Butter

Ranchero Beans

Curried Chickpea Stew

Mom's Chili

Bernadette's Beef Stew

Pork Chops and Potatoes for Two

Sausage in a Bun with Italian "Gravy"

Pork Loin Roast Cooked in Apple Cider

Sauerbraten

Lois's Slow-Cooked Brisket

Choucroute Garnie

Chicken Curry

Workday Chicken and Gravy

German-Style Red Cabbage

Buffet Potatoes

Super Sweet Potatoes

Shayna's Copper Pennies

Orange Marmalade Bread Pudding

Mrs. Ramsey's "Surprise"

Apple Pudding Cake

 lühwein

This is not an authentic recipe for German hot, spiced wine, but rather a simplified version that we've used for years. It's helped keep us warm sitting around a campfire, many a cold night.

5 cups apple cider

5 cups burgundy wine

½ cup honey

½ cup cinnamon red hots

Place all ingredients in slow cooker and stir to combine. Cover and cook on HIGH for 1 to 2 hours or on LOW 3 to 4 hours.

SERVES: 5

SLOW COOKER SIZE: 4 quart

PREP TIME: 5 minutes

COOKING TIME: 1 to 2 hours on HIGH or 3 to 4 hours on LOW

Serving Suggestions

Serve on a frosty night with grilled bratwurst or just a slice of apple strudel.

Variations

You could add a spice bag with whole cloves and allspice to add even more flavor. Try adding the rind of one lemon peeled in a spiral for additional sparkle.

Tip

Red wine can be a bear to clean up if you ever spill it on yourself or a light-colored carpet. Should that happen, attack the spot right away with either club soda or salt to help pull the stain out of the fabric.

Caponata

See our serving suggestions to turn this appetizer into a quick meal or salad.
Our favorite way to enjoy this relish is on top of grilled pizza dough.

1 eggplant (about 1 pound), peeled and cut into ³/₄-inch cubes

1 teaspoon salt

¹/₂ yellow or orange bell pepper, cut into ¹/₂-inch pieces

3 plum tomatoes, diced

2 medium carrots, cut into ¹/₂-inch slices

2 plum tomatoes, diced

1 medium onion, peeled and chopped

1 large garlic clove, peeled and minced

2 tablespoons lightly toasted pine nuts

3 tablespoons tomato paste

1 teaspoon sugar

2 tablespoons fresh lemon juice

2 tablespoons olive oil

2 tablespoons drained capers

¹/₂ cup kalamata olives, pitted and chopped

3 tablespoons chopped fresh flat-leafed parsley leaves

Salt and pepper to taste

1 tablespoon lemon juice, optional

Pita bread cut into wedges

1. In a large colander, toss the eggplant with salt. Allow to drain for 1 hour. Rinse well under cold water and drain.

2. Place all ingredients except the capers, olives, and parsley in slow cooker.

SERVES: 8 to 10

SLOW COOKER SIZE: 4 quart

PREP TIME: 20 minutes

COOKING TIME: 7 to 8 hours on LOW

Serving Suggestions

Generously oil small rounds of pizza dough, place them on a hot grill, grill each side about 3 to 4 minutes until browned, then top with the caponata. You could also serve this relish over pasta or cooked beans such as garbanzos, as a hot or cold meal or salad, or as an omelet filling; it's also great as a condiment for simple grilled meat of fish. It's especially good taken along on a picnic as a sandwich filling.

Variations

To lighten, reduce the olive oil to 2 teaspoons and omit the olives.

Tip

Eggplant can be rather bitter tasting; salting the eggplant before cooking removes a great deal of the bitter liquid.

3. Cover and cook on LOW for 7 to 8 hours.

4. Stir in the capers, olives, and parsley. Season with salt and pepper and a little lemon juice, if desired. Refrigerate caponata for several hours or overnight.

5. Bring caponata to room temperature and serve with wedges of pita bread.

To pit kalamata olives, pound sharply with the flat side of a large knife blade to split them open.

$\mathcal{S}$pinach Dip Ahoy!

We resurrected this oldie but goodie from our recipe files and adapted it for the slow cooker. They'll come from the four corners of the world when you serve this as an appetizer!

2 (10-ounce) packages frozen, chopped spinach
½ cup butter
2 medium onions, chopped
¼ cup flour
1 cup evaporated milk
1 tablespoon Worcestershire sauce
3 cups (12 ounces) pepper jack cheese, cut into cubes
1½ teaspoons celery salt
2 or 3 cloves garlic, minced
1 teaspoon pepper
Tortilla chips, crackers, fresh vegetables, or toasted bread cubes for dipping

SERVES: 12
SLOW COOKER SIZE: 1½ quart
PREP TIME: 25 minutes
COOKING TIME: 2 hours on LOW

Serving Suggestions

Serve this warm appetizer right out of the slow cooker set on WARM or LOW to keep it warm.

Variations

To lighten, use half the butter, evaporated skim milk, and reduced fat cheese

Tip

If you can't find reduced-fat pepper jack cheese, use reduced-fat Monterey jack cheese and stir in a 4-ounce can of diced green chilies or jalapeño peppers.

1. Following the package directions, cook the spinach then drain very well, reserving ½ cup of the liquid.

2. In a large Dutch oven over MEDIUM heat, melt the butter. Add the onions and sauté until soft, about 3 minutes.

3. Stir flour into onion mixture and cook for about 1 minute. Stir in evaporated milk, reserved spinach liquid, and Worcestershire sauce. Increase heat to MEDIUM-HIGH and cook, stirring constantly, until the sauce comes to a boil and thickens.

4. Place the rest of ingredients in slow cooker and stir in the sauce to combine. Cover and cook on LOW for 2 hours until the cheese melts. Stir and serve warm with tortilla chips, crackers, fresh vegetables, or toasted bread cubes.

$\mathcal{M}$aria's Tortilla

Most of us know tortillas as flat bread made from wheat or corn flour. In Spain a tortilla is a combination of potatoes, onions, and eggs cooked in a large skillet. Try our slow cooker version of that popular dish some Sunday evening when you feel like breakfast for dinner.

2 pounds potatoes (about 3 large) peeled and cut into $^1/_8$-inch-thick slices

1 large onion, peeled and thinly sliced

$^1/_4$ cup butter, melted

12 eggs

Salt and pepper to taste

Hot pepper sauce or a chunky salsa

1. Place potatoes and onion in slow cooker; stir in melted butter. Cover and cook on HIGH for 2 hours.

2. Gently stir, then reduce heat to LOW.

3. In a large bowl, whisk together the eggs, salt, and pepper. Pour over the partially cooked potato mixture. Cook uncovered on LOW for 4 hours more, until the eggs are cooked in the center. Serve with a bottle of hot pepper sauce or a good salsa.

SERVES: 6	
SLOW COOKER SIZE: 4 quart	
PREP TIME: 20 minutes total	
COOKING TIME: 2 hours on HIGH, 4 hours on LOW	

Serving Suggestions

Serve with a ham steak, grilled or pan-fried in a little butter, and a glass of pink grapefruit juice.

Variations

Sometimes we like to add diced green chiles or a combination of chopped green and red peppers to this dish. To lighten the dish, substitute 2 cups (16 ounces) Egg Beaters for 8 of the eggs, and reduce the amount of melted butter to 2 tablespoons.

Tip

Some slow cookers have hot spots. If yours does, rotate the liner a few times during cooking to insure even cooking of the egg mixture.

Slow-Cooked Oatmeal

Not being fans of cooked oatmeal, we didn't have high hopes for this experiment. We were pleasantly surprised to find this very flavorful hot cereal something we'd make again. Best of all, you can cook it overnight and have a hot breakfast ready for you and your family the minute you roll out of bed!

3 cups steel cut oats (Irish oats) (see Tip)

1 cup dried apple slices

¼ cup brown sugar

1 tablespoon cinnamon, or to taste

¼ teaspoon salt

4 cups water

4 cups apple juice or cider

Place all ingredients in slow cooker and stir to combine. Cover and cook on LOW overnight for 6 to 8 hours.

SERVES: 6 1-cup servings	
SLOW COOKER SIZE: 4 quart	
PREP TIME: 7 minutes	
COOKING TIME: 6 to 8 hours on LOW	

Serving Suggestions

For breakfast on the run, serve this hot with an ice cold glass of milk. Or you can serve a smaller portion as part of a hearty breakfast of bacon, eggs, and orange juice.

Variations

The combinations of dried fruit and juices you could substitute for the dried apple and apple juice are almost endless. Try dried apricots and apricot nectar, dried bananas and pineapple juice, dried cherries and cranberry juice, dates and apple juice, dried peaches and peach nectar.

Tip

You don't want to substitute instant oatmeal in this dish. The regular oats are okay, but the steel-cut oats hold up best of all.

$\mathcal{B}$eef-Bean-and-Barley Soup

This simple soup is one you can easily add to or subtract from. For vegetarians, omit the beef. For vegetable lovers, add carrots, parsnips, turnips, peppers, etc. Let your imagination be your guide.

1½ pounds beef stew meat, cut into bite-size pieces

1 (16-ounce) can cannellini beans, rinsed and drained

½ cup pearl barley, rinsed

4 cups fresh spinach, stemmed and chopped

2 cloves garlic, minced

3 cups vegetable or beef broth

1 (16-ounce) can diced tomatoes, undrained

1 large stalk celery, sliced

1 large onion, chopped

Salt and pepper to taste

1. Place all ingredients in slow cooker and stir to combine. Cover and cook on LOW for 6 to 8 hours.

2. Taste before serving. If necessary, reseason with a dash of salt, pepper, and any other flavors that may have cooked out.

SERVES: 6

SLOW COOKER SIZE: 4½ quart

PREP TIME: 10 minutees

COOKING TIME: 6 to 8 hours on LOW

Serving Suggestions

Serve with a salad of torn romaine and arugula sprinkled with thin slices of pear, some crumbled blue cheese and chopped toasted walnuts. For dessert you can splurge with a slice of chocolate cake.

Variations

For more flavor, you can brown the beef in 1 tablespoon oil before adding it to the slow cooker.

To save time, buy prewashed spinach in a bag.

Tip

Save time. Buy prewashed and trimmed spinach in bags.

Cream of Cauliflower Soup

This is a smooth, creamy soup that would make an elegant first course for a special meal.

½ cup (1 stick) butter

1 tablespoon minced onion

1 tablespoon minced celery

½ cup flour

6½ cups homemade chicken broth (or four 14-ounce cans)

1½ teaspoons salt

½ teaspoon pepper

1 head cauliflower, leaves removed, quartered, and core removed

½ cup heavy cream

1. In a large saucepan, melt the butter over LOW heat. Add onion and celery; sauté about 2 minutes, until slightly softened.

2. Stir in flour, salt, and pepper; cook about 2 minutes more, stirring occasionally.

3. Whisk in broth until smooth.

4. Carefully pour soup into slow cooker. Add cauliflower. Cover and cook on LOW for 6 hours. If desired, remove a few small pieces of cauliflower and set aside.

SERVES: 4 to 6

SLOW COOKER SIZE: 4 quart

PREP TIME: 20 minutes

COOKING TIME: 6 hours on LOW

Serving Suggestions

Serve proudly with broiled fish fillets or rack of lamb, curry rice, and grilled vegetables.

Variations

To lighten this recipe, cut the amount of butter in half and substitute ½ cup low fat milk for the cream.

If you prefer a thicker soup, add 1 cup instant potato flakes just before serving.

Tip

When pouring the heated contents of a skillet into the slow cooker pot, we suggest placing the slow cooker pot in the sink and pouring the contents of the skillet into it there. If you accidently spill, you'll avoid getting burned and clean up will be much easier.

5. With an immersion blender, blend the soup well until smooth and thickened. (Or process in small batches in a blender, then return to the slow
   cooker.)

6. Taste before serving. If necessary, reseason with a dash of salt, pepper, and
   any other flavors that may have cooked out. Stir in cream and reserved cauliflower. Serve.

ulashsuppe

Linda, her husband, and infant daughter lived in Germany for several years and still miss the hearty soups and breads served there. This goulash soup closely resembles one of their favorite meals at the local gasthaus. It's definitely worth the extra time it takes to brown the meat first. Yes, the recipe does call for three tablespoons of paprika. If you have trouble locating sweet Hungarian paprika, try this Web site: http://www.penzeys.com/cgi-bin/ penzeys/shophome.html

3 tablespoons vegetable oil

1 pound boneless beef chuck roast, trimmed and
   cut into bite-size pieces

¼ cup flour

Salt and pepper to taste

2 tablespoons vegetable oil

2 onions, peeled and chopped

1 large stalk celery, chopped

1 teaspoon caraway seeds

3 tablespoons sweet Hungarian paprika

4 cups homemade beef stock (or three 10-ounce
   cans of beef broth)

2 medium potatoes, peeled and cut into ½-inch
   cubes

3 carrots, peeled and cut into ½-inch cubes

2 bay leaves

2 tablespoons tomato paste

¼ teaspoon hot red pepper sauce

3 tablespoons red wine vinegar

1 teaspoon dried thyme

1 teaspoon salt

1. In a large nonstick skillet, heat the 3 table-spoons oil over MEDIUM heat.

SERVES: 6

SLOW COOKER SIZE:
4 quart

PREP TIME: 50 minutes

COOKING TIME: 8 to 10 hours
on LOW

Serving Suggestions

This soup is even better the second day. Serve with large, crusty rolls for bowl mopping.

Variations

You could add 1 chopped green pepper in the last half hour, if desired. You could also top each bowl of soup with a dollop of sour cream.

Tip

When pouring the heated contents of a skillet into the slow cooker pot, we suggest placing the slow cooker pot in the sink and pouring the contents of the skillet into it there. If you accidently

2. Meanwhile, in a pie plate combine the flour and salt and pepper to taste. Dredge the meat in the flour mixture and shake off the excess flour.

3. Add the meat to the hot oil in two batches. Brown well on all sides, then remove and place in the slow cooker pot.

4. Add 2 tablespoons more oil to the skillet. Stir in the onions, celery, caraway seeds, and paprika. Cook and stir until the onions are soft, about 5 minutes.

5. Pour 1 cup of the beef broth into the skillet, stirring to remove all the cooked browned bits from the bottom of the pan. Pour mixture into the slow cooker pot.

6. Add the rest of the ingredients to the slow cooker, including the remaining 3 cups beef broth. Stir to combine.

7. Cover and cook on LOW for 8 to 10 hours.

8. Taste before serving. If necessary, reseason with a dash of salt, pepper, and any other flavors that may have been diluted during cooking. Remove the bay leaves before serving.

spill, you'll avoid getting burned and clean up will be much easier.

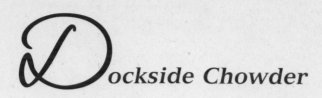ockside Chowder

This easy-to-prepare main course soup is down-home good! You might even make a fish lover out of a finicky eater with this recipe.

8 strips bacon, diced into ½ inch pieces

1 onion, finely chopped

2 stalks celery, sliced

2 cloves garlic, minced

6 tablespoons flour

2 teaspoons salt

1 teaspoon pepper

4 cups water

4 large russet potatoes

1 pound firm white fish such as cod, diced into
   1-inch pieces

1½ cups heavy cream

2 teaspoons dried thyme

4 dashes hot sauce, such as Tabasco

4 dashes Worcestershire sauce

1. In a large, deep skillet or Dutch oven over medium heat, cook the bacon until almost crisp, about 7 minutes. Add the onion and celery and cook until the onion is soft, about 3 minutes more.

2. Add garlic, flour, and salt and pepper. Stir and cook about 1 minute more.

3. Deglaze the pan by adding the water, bringing the mixture to a boil and scraping any browned bits off the bottom of the pan. Set aside.

SERVES: 8	
SLOW COOKER SIZE: 4 quart	
PREP TIME: 25 minutes	
COOKING TIME: 6 to 8 hours on LOW	

Serving Suggestions

Serve with homemade biscuits made from scratch or a mix, and a cherry cobbler for dessert.

Variations

You can use any firm white fish, such as seabass, cod, grouper, orange roughy, red snapper, mahi mahi, or halibut.

To lighten, replace the bacon with 1 tablespoon olive oil and substitute 1% milk for the cream.

Tip

When pouring the heated contents of a skillet into the slow cooker pot, we suggest placing the slow cooker pot on a towel in the sink and pouring the contents of the skillet into it there. If you accidently spill, you'll avoid getting burned and clean up will be much easier.

4. Peel and dice the potatoes into approximately ½-inch cubes.

5. Place the skillet contents and the potatoes into the slow cooker. Cover and cook on LOW for 6 to 8 hours until the potatoes are tender.

6. Add the fish, cream, thyme, hot sauce, and Worcestershire sauce, stirring gently. Cover and cook 30 minutes more.

7. Taste before serving. If necessary, reseason with a dash of salt, pepper, and any other flavors that may have cooked out. Serve hot.

Hot Beef Borscht

Great borscht achieves a perfect balance of sweet and sour flavors. Try our recipe and see what you think. You can always adjust the amounts of sugar and lemon juice to suit your own taste. A word of caution: the beet juices leave permanent stains on clothing and light counter surfaces. Handle with care.

1 tablespoon vegetable oil

1 (1-pound) bone-in beef shank

1 onion, thinly sliced

3 cloves garlic, minced

2 carrots, peeled and thinly sliced

2 large or 3 medium beets, peeled and chopped in a
   food processor

4 cups water

1 tablespoon concentrated beef broth base or
   3 beef bouillon cubes

1 tablespoon tomato paste

1 large russet potato, peeled, cut into ½-inch cubes

2 cups shredded cabbage

7 tablespoons brown sugar

7 tablespoons lemon juice

¼ cup chopped fresh dill

Salt and pepper to taste, if needed

Sour cream, to garnish

SERVES: 6
SLOW COOKER SIZE: 4½ quart
PREP TIME: 35 minutes
COOKING TIME: 6 to 8 hours on LOW

Serving Suggestions

A good Russian dark rye bread is a must with this rustic soup.

This Eastern European specialty is even better the day after it's made.

Variations

Substitute 2 pounds short ribs for the beef shank.

Substitute 1 parsnip for the carrots.

Substitute red wine vinegar for the lemon juice.

Use an immersion blender to puree soup before serving.

Tip

For more flavor, you could roast beets in the oven first by

1. Heat oil in large saucepan over medium-high heat. Add the beef shank and brown well on all sides. Remove and place in the slow cooker

2. Place the rest of the ingredients, except fresh dill, salt, pepper, and sour cream, in slow

cooker and stir to combine. Cover and cook on LOW for 6 to 8 hours.

3. When done, remove and discard the beef bone, shred the meat and return to the soup.

4. Taste before serving. If necessary, reseason with a dash of salt, pepper, and any other flavors that may have cooked out. You can either stir in the dill at the end or sprinkle some on top of each serving, along with a dollop of sour cream.

wrapping in foil and baking at 375°F for one hour.

Beets will stain your hands. It's best to wear gloves while working with them.

$\mathcal{S}$low Cooker Fondue

Skip the hassle of expensive fondue pots and special fuels. A small 1½-quart slow cooker is the perfect vehicle for delicious fondue!

1 large clove garlic, cut in half
1 cup evaporated milk
½ cup dry white wine or sparkling cider
¼ to ½ teaspoon bottled hot pepper sauce, optional
2 tablespoons flour
½ teaspoon dry mustard
2 cups Swiss cheese, cubed
2 cups fontina cheese, cubed
1 (1-pound) loaf crusty French or Italian bread, cut into bite-size cubes

1. Rub inside of slow cooker with cut pieces of garlic.

2. Pour evaporated milk, wine, and hot pepper sauce into slow cooker. Stir to combine.

3. In a medium bowl, stir together the flour and dry mustard. Add the cheese cubes and toss in flour mixture until well coated. Add to slow cooker, stir, cover, and cook on LOW for 3 to 4 hours until heated through and the cheese has melted.

4. Whisk to combine. Serve in slow cooker set on WARM or LOW heat with bread cubes and fondue forks.

SERVES: 6
SLOW COOKER SIZE: 1½ quart
Prep: 15 minutes
COOKING TIME: 3 to 4 hours on LOW

Serving Suggestions

You can serve this with a platter of crudities of choice: cooked asparagus, colorful bell pepper strips, broccoli and/or cauliflower florets, carrots, snow peas, radishes, jicama, or pickle spears. Consider them a side dish, but they are also good for dipping in the fondue.

Variations

Vary the types of cheese as you please.

For a romantic meal, prepare a half recipe for two: whoever loses a piece of bread in the fondue has to pay up with a kiss.

Tip

Keep the slow cooker on WARM or LOW. Cheese will eventually coagulate into a big blob if heated too long or at too high a temperature.

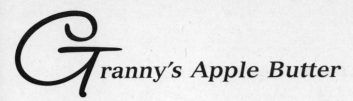 ranny's Apple Butter

The granny in this recipe is Granny Smith and her apples. When you make your own apple butter, you can serve it warm right out of the slow cooker or freeze or can it for later use. It's especially good slathered over a slice of homemade whole grain bread, fresh from the bread machine. Make this when you're home for the day. It fills the house with a glorious aroma.

8 large Granny Smith apples, peeled, cored, and
   quartered
½ cup apple juice or cider
¾ cup dark brown sugar
2 teaspoons ground cinnamon
½ teaspoon ground allspice
½ teaspoon ground cloves

1. Place apples and juice in slow cooker. Cover and cook on HIGH for 4 hours until the apples are very soft.

2. Stir in the remaining ingredients and cook 2 hours more, *uncovered,* stirring occasionally. When done, puree with an immersion blender. Serve warm or refrigerate.

Yields: 3 cups
SLOW COOKER SIZE: 4 quart
PREP TIME: 40 minutes
COOKING TIME: 6 hours on HIGH

Serving Suggestions

This is good on toast, or try it on pancakes or warm gingerbread.

Variations

For apple-pear butter, substitute 4 peeled and cored pears for 4 of the apples.

Tip

The easiest way to core apples and pears is to cut them in half and remove the cores with a melon baller.

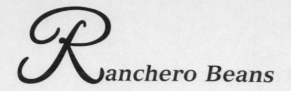anchero Beans

These smoky beans will be welcome at any potluck or barbeque. Wrap the crockery pot in newspaper and a heavy beach towel to transport it and the beans will stay warm until you're ready to eat.

6 slices bacon

1 large onion, chopped

1 (8-ounce) can tomato sauce

1 cup dark brown sugar

1 tablespoon Worcestershire sauce

1 tablespoon molasses

1 tablespoon cider vinegar

½ teaspoon liquid smoke

1 tablespoon chili powder

½ teaspoon crushed red pepper flakes

1 teaspoon salt

2 (15-ounce) cans kidney beans, drained and rinsed

2 (15-ounce) cans pinto beans, drained and rinsed

1 (15-ounce) can garbanzo beans, drained and rinsed

1 (15-ounce) can black beans, drained and rinsed

SERVES: 6
SLOW COOKER SIZE: 4 quart
PREP TIME: 30 minutes
COOKING TIME: 4 to 6 hours on LOW

Serving Suggestions

Serve with baked or grilled ham, fresh pineapple spears, and coconut cake for dessert.

Variations

You can vary the types of beans as desired.

If you're a vegetarian or feeding one, just omit the bacon and substitute about 1 tablespoon oil.

Tip

Save time and dump all 6 cans of beans into one large colander to rinse and drain.

1. In a large nonstick skillet, over medium heat, cook the bacon until crisp. Drain on paper towels, and when cool crumble and place in slow cooker.

2. Pour off the grease but do not wash the skillet. Sauté the onion in same skillet until soft, about 3 minutes. Add to slow cooker.

3. Place rest of ingredients in slow cooker and stir to combine. Cover and cook on LOW for 4 to 6 hours.

Curried Chickpea Stew

This Indian-inspired dish is a nice break from traditional beef and potato stews. If you have vegetarians coming for dinner, this dish will please meat eaters and nonmeat eaters alike.

2 tablespoons olive oil

1 large onion, peeled and chopped

4 large cloves garlic, minced

3 stalks celery, sliced ½-inch thick

4 (15-ounce) cans garbanzo beans, rinsed and drained

3 tablespoons curry powder

¼ teaspoon cayenne pepper

Salt and pepper to taste

1 tablespoon lemon juice

2 (14-ounce) cans chicken or vegetable broth

2 tablespoons chopped fresh parsley

SERVES: 6

SLOW COOKER SIZE: 4 quart

PREP TIME: 20 minutes

COOKING TIME: 6 to 8 hours on LOW

Serving Suggestions

Pita bread cut in half or quarters, toasted or untoasted, would be a good accompaniment.

A strawberry and spinach salad or some sliced home-grown tomatoes would also go well with this stew. And a dish of peppermint ice cream would round out this light meal.

Variations

To add a tomato flavor, substitute 1 (16-ounce) can diced tomatoes in puree for 1 can of the broth.

Tip

Curry powder isn't just one spice but rather various combinations of spices. It pays to shop around and do some taste testing until you find the curry powder you like best.

1. In a nonstick skillet, heat the oil over medium heat. Add the onions and sauté until soft, about 3 minutes. Add the garlic and cook 1 minute more.

2. Place all ingredients except the chopped parsley in slow cooker, and stir to combine. Cover and cook on LOW for 6 to 8 hours.

3. Taste before serving. If necessary, reseason with a dash of salt, pepper, and any other flavors that may have cooked out. Garnish with chopped parsley and serve.

$\mathcal{M}$om's Chili

Linda's mom was a great cook—but her family still laughs at the time she switched the quantities of cayenne and chili in this recipe. That was one unforgettable bowl of chili!

2 cups dry kidney beans

1½ pounds round steak or beef stew meat, trimmed of fat and cut into 1½-inch pieces

1 (28-ounce) can whole tomatoes, drained, cut into pieces

1 large onion, chopped

1 green pepper, chopped

1 clove garlic, minced

3 tablespoons chili powder

1 teaspoon cayenne pepper

1 teaspoon salt

1. The night before, place the beans in a bowl and add water to cover by about 2 inches. Soak overnight.

2. The following morning, drain the beans. Place all ingredients in the slow cooker, except the salt, and stir to combine. Cover and cook on LOW for 10 to 12 hours.

3. Just before serving, stir in the salt.

SERVES: 6

SLOW COOKER SIZE:
4½ quart

PREP TIME: 20 minutes

COOKING TIME: 10 to 12 hours on LOW

Serving Suggestions

Serving just a bowl of this chili with a side of cornbread will leave room for a luscious dessert such as lemon meringue pie.

Variations

If your chili powder is especially hot, you may want to start with just two tablespoons in this recipe, adding more after tasting, if desired.

If you prefer a chili with more tomato flavor, you can stir in one 15-ounce can of tomato sauce at the end and heat through.

For a good chili mac, cook 8 ounces of macaroni and stir into the chili just before serving.

To skip the overnight bean soak, substitute 2 (15-ounce) cans of drained and rinsed kidney beans for the dried, adding them the last hour of cooking.

 Tips

Drain the tomatoes, leave them in the can, and then use kitchen shears to cut them up into small pieces.

You'll find it easier to cut up the steak if you partially freeze it first.

*B*ernadette's Beef Stew

"Mother-in-Law's Stew" would be another name for this one because Linda's mother-in-law Bernadette shared this family recipe with her when she was a young bride. Now we've turned it into a slow cooker recipe.

2 pounds stew meat or chuck roast, cut into 1-inch pieces

4 large carrots, peeled and cut into bite-size chunks

4 stalks celery, cut into bite-size chunks

4 medium russet potatoes, peeled, cut into bite-size chunks

1 medium onion, cut into bite-size chunks

2 cloves garlic, peeled and minced

1 (15-ounce) can tomato sauce

1½ teaspoons salt

½ teasoon pepper

2 tablespoons dry quick-cooking tapioca

1 (15-ounce) can green beans, drained or
   1 (16-ounce) package frozen green beans

1. Place all ingredients, except green beans, in slow cooker and stir to combine. Cover and cook on LOW for 8 to 10 hours. Add green beans and cook 30 minutes more.

2. Taste before serving. If necessary, reseason with a dash of salt, pepper, and any other flavors that may have cooked out.

SERVES: 4

SLOW COOKER SIZE: 4 quart

PREP TIME: 30 minutes

COOKING TIME: 8 to 10 hours on LOW

Serving Suggestions

Serve with a small green salad and sourdough biscuits. For dessert, scoop out the center of two fresh pears and stuff each half with some crumbled blue cheese. Serve with a couple of sugar wafer cookies.

Variations

If you have a 6-to 7-quart cooker and need to feed six, increase meat to 3 pounds and use 6 each of carrots, celery, and potatoes.

When you add the green beans, you can also add any herb of choice to this basic stew, such as rosemary, oregano, dill, tarragon, thyme, or parsley.

Tip

Tapioca thickens the stew, it can be found in the pudding and gelatin section of most supermarkets.

Pork Chops and Potatoes for Two

When it's just dinner for two, try this tasty dish to warm you through and through.

2 tablespoons vegetable oil

2 pork chops with bone, each about 3/4-inch thick

2 tablespoons flour

2 tablespoons dry onion soup mix

1 cup water

2 large russet potatoes, sliced

1/2 large onion, peeled and sliced

Salt and pepper to taste

1. Heat oil in a large skillet over MEDIUM-HIGH heat. Add pork chops and brown lightly, about 4 minutes per side. Remove and set aside.

2. Reduce heat to medium. To the remaining oil in the skillet, whisk in the flour and onion soup mix and cook 1 minute. Whisk in water and bring to a boil, stirring until gravy thickens and comes to a boil.

3. Place potatoes and onion in slow cooker, pour gravy on top, and stir to combine. Place pork chops on top. Cover and cook on LOW for 6 to 8 hours until tender.

4. Taste before serving. Season with salt and pepper, if necessary.

SERVES: 2

SLOW COOKER SIZE: 4 quart

PREP TIME: 15 minutes

COOKING TIME: 6 to 8 hours on LOW

Serving Suggestions

Add color to this dish by serving it with sautéed green, red, and yellow bell pepper strips. Create a simple ambrosia for dessert by combining some mandarin oranges, green grapes, a drizzle of honey and a sprinkle of sweetened shredded coconut in a small compote dish.

Pour some cold ginger ale over all and serve.

Variations

To serve four, double the recipe and cook in a 6-quart slow cooker.

Tip

Because pork chops are now so lean, it's easy to overcook them until they're tough and dried out. This moist, slow-cooking method helps keep them juicy and tender.

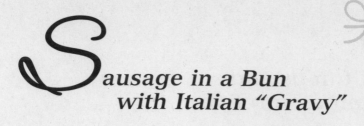

Sausage in a Bun
with Italian "Gravy"

When Italian sausages are slow-cooked in tomato sauce like this they are out-of-this-world, melt-in-your-mouth good! Mark this recipe with a star, because we guarantee you'll want to return to it again and again.

2 (28-ounce) cans tomato puree

1 onion, peeled and chopped

2 cloves garlic, peeled and minced

$\frac{1}{2}$ pound button mushrooms, cleaned and sliced

$\frac{1}{2}$ cup dry red wine, optional

$\frac{1}{4}$ cup dried parsley

2 tablespoons dried basil

1 tablespoon dried oregano

1 teaspoon sugar

2 teaspoons salt

$\frac{1}{2}$ teaspoon pepper

1 tablespoon olive oil

2 pounds (about 12) hot or mild Italian sausages

1 dozen soft or hard sandwich buns or French rolls

SERVES: 10 to 12

SLOW COOKER SIZE: 4 quart

PREP TIME: 25 minutes

COOKING TIME: 6 to 8 hours on LOW

Serving Suggestions

Serve with a side of pasta salad or oven-baked garlic fries. Cut 10 to 12 russet potatoes into wedges, toss with about 3 tablespoons olive oil and 6 minced cloves garlic. Season with salt and pepper, place on two rimmed baking sheets, on upper and lower racks in the oven, and bake at 450°F for 40 to 45 minutes, turning once, until brown and crispy.

(You'll need to alternate baking sheets in the oven halfway through, so both brown.)

Variations

To lighten, substitute turkey sausages, but cook only 2 hours in the sauce.

This recipe makes plenty of sauce. Freeze it for later use as a pasta sauce, or toss some

1. Combine all but the last 3 ingredients in the slow cooker to form the sauce. Stir well, cover, and cook on LOW for 3 hours.

2. In a nonstick skillet over MEDIUM heat, cook the sausages in the oil until brown on all sides, about 8 minutes. Add to slow cooker, cover, and cook 3 to 5 more hours.

3. Taste before serving. If necessary, reseason with a dash of salt, pepper, and any other fla-

vors that may have cooked out. Serve sausages on buns with a little sauce on top. Freeze any leftover sauce for future use.

meatballs into it and you'll have the makings of meatball sandwiches the following day.

Tip

If you don't have room in the freezer for leftover sauce, just cut the sauce ingredients in half when making this recipe.

*P*ork Loin Roast Cooked in Apple Cider

The combination of pork roast, tangy applesauce, and potato pancakes is a real taste treat! Try it.

2 tablespoons oil

1 (4-pound) boneless pork loin, trimmed of fat

1 cup apple cider

¼ cup Dijon mustard

2 teaspoons dried thyme or rosemary

2 tablespoons light brown sugar

APPLESAUCE:

4 cups unsweetend applesauce

2 tablespoon prepared horseradish

4 teaspoons light brown sugar

2 teaspoon fresh lemon juice

1. Heat oil in a Dutch oven over medium heat. Brown roast on all sides, about 8 minutes per side. Remove from pan.

2. Pour cider in bottom of slow cooker.

3. In a small bowl, combine the mustard, thyme, and brown sugar. Brush all of the sauce over the roast and carefully place in slow cooker.

4. Cover and cook on LOW for 6 to 8 hours.

5. Meanwhile, in a medium saucepan over MEDIUM heat, combine the applesauce ingre-

SERVES: 8
SLOW COOKER SIZE: 4 quart
PREP TIME: 15 minutes
COOKING TIME: 6 to 8 hours on LOW

Serving Suggestions

While you wait for the roast to finish cooking, whip up some potato pancakes by combining 6 cups grated raw potato, ½ cup grated onion, ⅔ cup milk, 4 beaten eggs, 6 tablespoons flour, and salt and pepper to taste. Drop by spoonfuls onto greased griddle or large skillet over MEDIUM heat. Brown both sides well and keep warm in oven.

Some peas and carrots would be a good side dish to add color to the plate.

Variations

To save time, you can omit step 1.

Tip

If your brown sugar is rock hard, you can microwave it

dients and stir until heated through. Remove from heat and allow to cool to room temperature.

6. When roast is done, remove from slow cooker, let it rest 5 to 10 minutes, then slice and serve with applesauce on the side.

10 to 15 seconds to help soften it up again.

$\mathcal{S}$auerbraten

To do it right, sauerbraten really needs to marinate for several days in the refrigerator. But you can cut the time by a day or two and it will still taste very good! Start the marinade at least one hour in advance, to give it time to cool before pouring it over the roast.

1½ cups apple juice or apple cider

1½ cups red wine vinegar

1 onion, peeled and sliced

2 bay leaves

15 whole cloves

1 teaspoon salt

¼ teaspoon pepper

1 (4-pound) boneless chuck, rump, or sirloin tip
   roast, trimmed of fat

½ cup crushed gingersnaps

Salt and pepper to taste

1. At least one hour ahead of time, place the first 7 ingredients in saucepan and bring to a boil over MEDIUM-HIGH heat. Reduce heat to low and simmer for 10 minutes. This step could be done the day before.

2. Place the roast in a zip-top plastic bag or small bowl and pour the marinade over it (liquid should cover meat). Seal or cover and refrigerate at least overnight, or up to 3 days, turning occasionally.

3. Remove roast from marinade, strain the marinade and reserve 1½ cups of the strained

---

SERVES: 6

SLOW COOKER SIZE: 4 quart

PREP TIME: 25 minutes

**COOKING TIME: 6 to 8 hours
on LOW**

Serving Suggestions

Serve with roasted potatoes, German-Style Red Cabbage (see page 175), and a colorful vegetable such as steamed carrots. A small slice of apple strudel from a local bakery would be the perfect ending to this authentic German meal.

To roast potatoes, toss peeled and quartered potatoes with 1 to 2 tablespoons olive oil, salt and pepper to taste, and optional fresh herbs of choice, such as fresh thyme or rosemary. Roast in 450°F oven for 25 to 30 minutes, stirring occasionally.

Variations

Before adding the roast to the slow cooker, you could pat it dry with paper towels, dust it with a little flour, and then brown it

marinade. Place roast in slow cooker. Add re-served marinade, cover, and cook on LOW for 6 to 8 hours. When tender, remove roast from slow cooker and keep warm.

4. Pour 2 cups of the cooking liquid into a small saucepan over MEDIUM-HIGH heat. Add crushed gingersnaps and season to taste with salt and pepper. Bring to a boil and cook until the crumbs have dissolved and thickened the gravy.

5. Slice roast across the grain and serve with gingersnap gravy.

well on all sides in a Dutch oven with a tablespoon or two of hot oil.

Tip

Crush the gingersnaps in a food processor until fine crumbs. If not finely crushed, they will add lumps to the gravy.

$\mathcal{L}$ois's Slow-Cooked Brisket

Lois knows brisket, and here's one of her favorite ways to prepare it.

1½ teaspoons salt

1½ teaspoons pepper

2 teaspoons dried thyme

3 carrots, peeled and sliced ¼-inch thick

1 (4-pound) flat or first-cut brisket, trimmed of fat

3 tablespoons vegetable oil

7 cloves garlic, minced

4 large onions, peeled and sliced

½ cup homemade or canned beef broth

¼ cup tomato paste

1 cup dry red wine

½ cup apricot nectar

1. In a small bowl, combine the salt, pepper, and thyme.

2. Place the carrots in the bottom of the slow cooker and season with a pinch or two of the salt mixture.

3. Sprinkle a generous portion of the salt mixture on both sides of the brisket.

4. In a large skillet, heat 2 tablespoons oil on MEDIUM-HIGH heat. Add the brisket and brown well on both sides. (Cut brisket in half, if necessary, to fit in the skillet.) Remove and place in slow cooker.

SERVES: 8	
SLOW COOKER SIZE: 6 quart	
PREP TIME: 35 minutes	
COOKING TIME: 10 to 12 hours on LOW	

Serving Suggestions

Serve with steamed brussels sprouts and either potato pancakes and applesauce or smashed potatoes: Boil 4 pounds unpeeled red new potatoes until tender, about 20 minutes. Drain well and add 1 cup milk, 6 tablespoons butter, salt and pepper to taste. With a fork or potato masher, partially mash the potatoes, incorporating all the milk and butter.

When leftover brisket has cooled, slice across the grain. Place slices in the gravy and refrigerate overnight. It's even better warmed up the next day.

Variations

To save time (but lose flavor), skip steps 4 and 5 and just place all ingredients in slow cooker without browning the meat first.

5. In the same skillet on medium heat, add 1 more tablespoon of oil, if needed, and sauté the onions until soft, about 4 minutes. Add garlic and cook 1 minute more. Sprinkle the rest of the salt mixture on top. Pour onions and garlic on top of the brisket.

6. Off heat, whisk together the broth, tomato paste, and apricot nectar in the skillet. Pour over the brisket. Cover and cook on LOW for 10 to 12 hours until fork tender.

7. To serve, slice brisket thinly across the grain. Skim any fat off the gravy and season to taste with salt and pepper, if necessary. Cover brisket with gravy and serve.

You can cut this recipe in half and cook in a 4-quart slow cooker.

Tip

There are two cuts of brisket. The first cut is called the "flat cut" and has less fat. The second cut is thicker and is called the "point cut."

$\mathcal{C}$houcroute Garnie
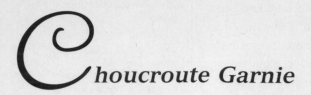

Don't be intimidated by the name. This rustic French dish is really just a sausage, sauerkraut, and vegetable casserole. So when the leaves start to fall and it's time to light that first fire in the fireplace, this hearty meal will warm you up right down to your tootsies.

8 small red potatoes, quartered

4 carrots, peeled and cut into chunks

6 slices bacon, diced

2 onions, peeled and chopped

2 pounds assorted sausages, such as kielbasa, Polish sausage, linguisa, frankfurters, Italian sausage, bratwurst, etc., cut into 1½-inch pieces

1 (15-ounce) can, jar, or package of sauerkraut, rinsed and drained

2 Granny Smith apples, peeled, cored, and chopped

2 teaspoons caraway seeds

2 tablespoons light brown sugar

4 sprigs fresh parsley

2 sprigs fresh thyme

1 bay leaf

15 black peppercorns

1 cup dry white wine or chicken broth

Salt and pepper to taste

SERVES: 6

SLOW COOKER SIZE: 6 quart

PREP TIME: 50 minutes

COOKING TIME: 6 to 8 hours on LOW

Serving Suggestions

Serve this one-pot meal with a good rye bread and coarse-grain mustard. For the finale, pass a plate of fig bars and some seedless grapes.

Variations

Reduce the amounts of vegetables and sausages to adapt this recipe for your 4-quart slow cooker.

You could substitute Canadian bacon and pork spareribs cut into individual pieces for the sausages.

To simplify and speed up this recipe, omit the carrots, apples, bacon, and bouquet garni of herbs.

1. Place potatoes and carrots in bottom of slow cooker.

2. In a large nonstick skillet, cook the bacon until crispy. Remove with tongs; drain on paper towels. Pour off bacon grease and reserve.

3. In the same skillet, sauté the onion until soft, about 3 minutes. Place in slow cooker, along with the bacon.

4. In the same skillet, heat 1 tablespoon reserved bacon grease over medium heat and brown the sausage pieces on all sides, about 10 minutes. Remove with a slotted spoon and place on top of onions and bacon.

5. Layer sauerkraut and apples on top. Sprinkle with caraway seeds and brown sugar.

6. Make a bouquet garni (see Tip) of parsley, thyme, bay leaves, and peppercorns; bury in the sauerkraut.

7. Pour wine over all and season to taste with salt and pepper. Cover and cook on LOW for 6 to 8 hours. Remove and discard bouquet garni before serving.

Tip

To create a bouquet garni, cut a double thickness of cheesecloth into a 9-inch square. Lay fresh herbs and spices in the center, bring the four corners up and tie into a bag with kitchen twine, leaving a long strand so it will be easy to retrieve.

Chicken Curry

This is a fun dish to serve family style, especially if you can create a lazy Susan in the center of your table. Set the slow cooker pot right on the table with a big bowl of cooked rice and lots of little bowls of condiments. Everyone can help themselves and create their own masterpiece.

2 large potatoes, peeled and cut in chunks

1 small onion, chopped

2 carrots, peeled and cut in chunks

1 clove garlic, chopped

1 (14-ounce) can chicken broth or 1¾ cups
    homemade chicken broth

1 tablespoon curry powder

1 teaspoon salt

½ teaspoon pepper

6 chicken breasts, bone in

1 cup heavy cream

1 teaspoon curry powder, optional

6 cups cooked rice

OPTIONAL CONDIMENTS:

chopped peanuts

canned French-fried onion rings

shredded coconut

chutney

chopped hard-boiled eggs

crumbled cooked bacon

golden raisins

mandarin oranges

chopped green onions, green and white parts

1. Place potatoes, onion, carrots, garlic, broth,
   1 tablespoon curry powder, salt, pepper, and

SERVES: 6
SLOW COOKER SIZE: 6 quart
PREP TIME: 10 minutes
COOKING TIME: 5½ to 7½ hours on LOW

Serving Suggestions

Serve with steamed broccoli spears.

Variations

To lighten, omit the cream and substitute 1 more large potato in the beginning to help thicken the sauce later on.

The chicken bones add more flavor during cooking, but to save time you could substitute boneless, skinless chicken breasts.

Tip

If you don't have an immersion blender, pour the sauce into a regular blender in small batches to puree it. Be careful not to fill the blender more than ⅔ full with the hot liquid.

chicken in slow cooker and stir to combine. Cover and cook on LOW for 5 to 7 hours.

2. Remove chicken and any stray bones from the slow cooker and allow chicken to cool slightly.

3. With an immersion blender, puree the broth in the slow cooker.

4. Remove bones and skin from chicken and discard. Shred the chicken and return to the slow cooker.

5. Stir in the cream; add 1 teaspoon more curry powder, if desired. Cover and cook on LOW for 30 minutes more.

6. Serve over hot cooked rice with condiments of choice sprinkled on top.

Workday Chicken and Gravy

It doesn't get any easier than this!

4 skinless, boneless chicken breasts
1 can cream of mushroom soup
1 can cream of chicken soup

1. Place all ingredients in slow cooker and stir to combine.

2. Cover and cook on LOW heat for 4 to 6 hours.

SERVES: 4
SLOW COOKER SIZE: 4 quart
PREP TIME: 5 minutes
COOKING TIME: 4 to 6 hours on LOW

Serving Suggestions

Serve with creamy mashed potatoes and a green vegetable. For dessert, fill tall glasses or champagne flutes with diced fresh fruit or canned fruit cocktail and pour some sparkling cider, Champagne, or a clear soda over the fruit and top with a sprig of fresh mint.

Variations

You could substitute other creamy soups for a different flavor, such as tomato or cream of celery.

Tip

You can set this dish on a timer to start up to 2 hours later, but refrigerate the soups overnight and make sure the chicken is very cold before adding to the cooker.

German-Style Red Cabbage

This is a German specialty frequently served with sauerbraten or schnitzel and warm potato salad. It's a colorful side dish that goes well with so many things.

6 slices bacon, diced

¼ cup light brown sugar

½ cup beef broth or 1 beef bouillon and ½ cup water

3 tablespoons red wine vinegar

1 large head red cabbage, cored and shredded

1 onion, sliced

2 Granny Smith apples, peeled, cored and sliced

1 teaspoon caraway, fennel, or celery seeds

Salt and pepper to taste

1. In a large skillet over medium heat, cook bacon until almost crispy, about 5 minutes.

2. Stir in brown sugar. Add broth and vinegar, bring to a boil, scraping up browned bits from bottom of pan. Remove from heat.

3. Place rest of ingredients in slow cooker. Pour bacon and sauce over cabbage and stir to combine. Cover and cook on LOW for 5 to 6 hours.

4. Taste before serving. If necessary, reseason with a dash of salt, pepper, and any other flavors that may have cooked out.

SERVES: 8	
SLOW COOKER SIZE: 4 quart	
PREP TIME: 20 minutes	
COOKING TIME: 5 to 6 hours on LOW	

Serving Suggestions

This is a classic side dish for any German meal such as Sauerbraten (see page 166), wienerschnitzel, or grilled bratwurst. Serve with a second colorful vegetable, such as steamed carrots, sautéed spinach, or green beans.

Variations

To lighten, drain all bacon grease from pan before adding sugar.

Tip

Scrub apples in warm, soapy water to remove the wax coating.

$\mathcal{B}$uffet Potatoes

Low-calorie it's not, but this dish fills the bill when the craving for comfort food comes knocking.

1 (10-ounce) can cream of mushroom soup

1 pint sour cream

¼ cup milk

6 medium russet potatoes, peeled and sliced
   ¼-inch thick

Salt and pepper, to taste

1 onion, chopped

2 cloves garlic, minced

1 cup (4 ounces) grated cheddar cheese

1. In a bowl, combine soup, sour cream and milk; set aside.

2. Place half of potatoes in bottom of slow cooker. Season to taste with salt and pepper. Sprinkle half of onions and garlic on top. Pour half of sauce into pot. Repeat layers, finishing with sauce.

3. Cover and cook on LOW for 8 to 10 hours. Just before serving, sprinkle cheese on top, cover, and heat long enough to melt.

SERVES: 6

SLOW COOKER SIZE: 4 quart

PREP TIME: 30 minutes

COOKING TIME: 8 to 10 hours on LOW

Serving Suggestions

To complete the comfort meal theme, serve with meat loaf and green beans.

Variations

To lighten, substitute the reduced fat versions of the soup, sour cream, milk, and cheese.

You can also speed up the preparation by substituting a 30-ounce package of frozen hash browns for the potatoes.

Tip

If you need to slice the potatoes ahead of time, just keep them in very cold, salted water to retain their color.

$\mathcal{S}$uper *Sweet Potatoes*

If you like your sweet potatoes extra sweet, this is the recipe for you.

1/4 cup unsalted butter or margarine, softened

1/3 cup dark brown sugar

1/2 cup finely chopped walnuts, optional

2 teaspoons ground cinnamon

1/4 teaspoon freshly grated nutmeg

1 teaspoon salt

3 pounds (about 6 medium) dark orange sweet
   potatoes, peeled and sliced 1/4-inch thick

1/3 cup maple syrup

1. In a small bowl, mix together the butter, sugar, walnuts, cinnamon, nutmeg, and salt. Spread mixture over the bottom of the slow cooker pot.

2. Layer sliced potatoes on top. Drizzle the maple syrup over all.

3. Cover and cook on LOW for 5 to 7 hours.

4. Taste before serving. If necessary, reseason with a dash of salt and any other flavors that may have cooked out.

5. There are two ways to serve this dish: drain and serve as slices, or mash well with a potato masher or immersion blender and serve as mashed sweet potatoes.

SERVES: 6

SLOW COOKER SIZE: 4 quart

PREP TIME: 20 minutes

COOKING TIME: 5 to 7 hours
on LOW

Serving Suggestions

Serve with grilled pork chops and steamed brussels sprouts.

Variations

To cut the sweetness, you could substitute 1/2 cup freshly squeezed orange juice for the maple syrup.

Tip

Though we often refer to the dark orange sweet potatoes as yams, technically they're not yams but another variety of sweet potatoes.

Shayna's Copper Pennies

Linda's daughter Shayna went back for a third helping of these one Thanksgiving, so we knew we had to include them in the book. Her husband gives them a big thumbs up as well.

1 (10 ¾-ounce) can condensed tomato soup

½ cup sugar

3 tablespoons vegetable oil

2 teaspoons Worcestershire sauce

½ cup cider vinegar

1 teaspoon dry mustard

½ teaspoon salt

½ teaspoon pepper

2 pounds carrots, peeled, and sliced ¼-inch thick

1 onion, cut into small chunks

1 green pepper, seeded, cut into small chunks

2 stalks celery, sliced

1. In slow cooker combine soup, sugar, oil, Worcestershire sauce, vinegar, mustard, salt and pepper.

2. Add vegetables and stir to coat with sauce. Cover and cook on LOW for 4 hours.

3. Serve warm as a side dish or pour into a bowl and refrigerate overnight. Strain and serve cold as a salad. Reserve sauce to pour over any leftovers.

SERVES: 8

SLOW COOKER SIZE: 4 quart

PREP TIME: 20 minutes

COOKING TIME: 4 hours on LOW

Serving Suggestions

These carrots are the perfect side dish or salad for potlucks and picnics because they can be served cold, room temperature, or hot.

Variations

You can lighten this recipe by cutting the amount of sugar, oil, and vinegar in half.

Tip

For best results, try to cut vegetables such as these carrots in uniform slices so they all cook to the same degree of doneness.

$\mathcal{O}$range Marmalade Bread Pudding

Bread pudding is the ultimate comfort food, and orange marmalade is a fitting companion to this family favorite of ours.

1 tablespoon butter or cooking oil spray

1 pound hearty white or egg bread, cut into 1-inch
  cubes (about 12 cups)

1 (16-ounce) jar orange marmalade

1 cup whole milk

1 cup heavy cream

½ cup sugar

3 eggs

2 teaspoons vanilla extract

1. Butter or spray the bottom and sides of the slow cooker pot.

2. Place cubed bread in bottom of slow cooker. Pour the marmalade evenly over bread and gently stir to combine.

3. In a bowl, whisk together the milk, cream, sugar, eggs, and vanilla. Pour over all, cover, and cook on HIGH for 2 to 2½ hours, until fully cooked in the center. Serve warm.

SERVES: 8 to 10

SLOW COOKER SIZE: 4 quart

PREP TIME: 15 minutes

COOKING TIME: 2 to 2½ hours on HIGH

Serving Suggestions

Try this after a seafood dinner. You can gild the lily by topping with cream or good vanilla ice cream.

Variations

Try using different marmalades for slightly different flavors. English marmalade is more bitter in flavor and is considered by some people to be "the real thing."

Tip

Bread puddings soak up the most liquid if you use 2- or 3-day-old bread or leave it out overnight to dry out.

$\mathcal{M}$rs. Ramsey's "Surprise"

This is a dessert with a story—a good idea that didn't quite turn out as planned. Every year at Thanksgiving, for as long as they've known each other, Linda and her family have camped with Peggy Ramsey and her family in the mountains, braving the cold and snow for a real pioneer-type feast. One year Peggy ran across an old recipe for pumpkin custard that native Americans used to make. It called for filling a pumpkin with custard ingredients and burying it in the coals of a dying fire to cook for hours. Unfortunately, the coals must have been a little too hot—when everyone smelled burning pumpkin, they looked over just in time to see a molten eruption of gooey pumpkin custard oozing everywhere. It was a mess! We think it's time to resurrect this dessert, simplify it, and give it a try in the slow cooker.

1 medium pumpkin, approximately 3 pounds, just
   wide enough to fit inside your slow cooker
1 (4.4-ounce) package dry custard dessert mix
2½ cups whole milk
Dash each of cinnamon and nutmeg
2 cups water

SERVES: 4	
SLOW COOKER SIZE: 4 quart	
PREP TIME: 20 minutes	
COOKING TIME: 3 to 4 hours on LOW	

1. Cut off the top ⅛ of the pumpkin and set aside. Scrape out all seeds and membranes, being careful not to puncture the pumpkin shell. (You might also have to cut some of the stem off so it will fit inside the pot.) Set aside

2. In a large microwavable bowl, stir the custard mix into the milk. Microwave on HIGH 8 minutes until it boils, stirring every 3 minutes. Pour into the pumpkin, sprinkle with cinnamon and nutmeg, and replace the top.

Serving Suggestions

This custard dessert would go well with turkey sandwiches at a Halloween party.

Variations

A dash of allspice would also be a nice addition to this dessert.

Tip

If you're interested in cooking a pumpkin to purée, select a smaller, sweeter cooking pumpkin, not the large, rather tasteless variety always sold at Halloween for carving.

3. Pour water into the slow cooker and carefully place filled pumpkin in the pot. Cover and cook on LOW for 3 to 4 hours until the pumpkin meat is tender.

4. Carefully remove pot from slow cooker and allow pumpkin to cool to room temperature. Once the custard has set, you can serve right from the slow cooker, or remove, refrigerate for several hours, and serve cold. To serve, scoop out some of the soft pumpkin flesh along with the custard in each spoonful.

$\mathcal{CA}$pple Pudding Cake

This is the first slow cooker dessert recipe we tried; we'd never been interested in slow cooker desserts before, but we were hooked! Linda loves this dish because it closely resembles a favorite cake mix she discovered in Vancouver, Canada, one that she was never able to find stateside.

1 tablespoon butter or cooking oil spray

5 cups peeled and cored Granny Smith apples (about 5 apples), sliced about ¼-inch thick

¾ cup sugar

1½ teaspoons ground cinnamon

⅛ teaspoon ground nutmeg

6 tablespoons butter, softened

1¼ cups sugar

1¼ cups all-purpose flour

1½ teaspoons baking powder

¾ teaspoon ground cinnamon

¼ teaspoon ground cloves

¼ teaspoon salt

¾ cup milk

¾ cup apple cider

1 tablespoon cornstarch

Vanilla ice cream

SERVES: 6

SLOW COOKER SIZE: 4 quart

PREP TIME: 40 minutes

COOKING TIME: 2 to 3 hours on HIGH

Serving Suggestions

When serving, be sure to scoop up some of the apple mixture on the bottom.

Variations

Instead of ice cream, serve with cream or whipped cream

Tip

Cut down your prep time by purchasing one of those apple peelers that attach to your counter. It makes peeling, coring, and slicing apples a one-step operation.

1. Butter or spray the bottom and sides of the slow cooker pot.

2. In a large bowl, toss the apples with the ¾ cup sugar, 1½ teaspoons cinnamon, and the ground nutmeg. Pour into the slow cooker.

3. In a large mixing bowl, mix together the 6 tablespoons butter and 1¼ cups sugar with an electric mixer.

4. In a separate bowl, combine the flour, baking powder, ¾ teaspoon cinnamon, cloves, and salt. Alternately add it to the butter mixture with the milk, beating well after each addition. Beat 1 minute until smooth. Pour batter over the apples, spreading to fully cover.

5. In a saucepan, combine the apple cider and cornstarch. Bring to a boil over MEDIUM-HIGH heat, whisking constantly until thickened. Remove from heat and pour over the cake batter. *Do not stir.*

6. Cover and cook on HIGH for 2 to 3 hours until bubbly and the cake tests done with a toothpick. Serve straight from the pot. Scoop up the apple mixture on the bottom with each serving. Serve warm with vanilla ice cream.

Winter

Winter

Minty Hot Cocoa

Curried Nuts

Knockout Dip

Christmas Morning Baked Apples

Orange Marmalade Strata

Our Favorite Split Pea Soup

Taco Soup

Day-After Turkey Noodle Soup

Vegetable Chowder

Turkey-and-Dumplings Soup

Game Day Chowder

Crocked Cranberry Sauce

Baked Beans from Scratch

Chili and Cornbread

Chicken and Dumplings

Pat's Special Beef Stew

Sloppy Joes

Sloppy Janes

Curry Wurst

Barnetta's BBQ'd Ribs

Sweet-and-Sour Pork

Round Steak Smothered in Onions and Beer

Swiss Steaks and Gravy

Julie's Chicken

Lasagna

Savory Bread Stuffing

Turkey and Stuffing in a Pot

Winter Root Vegetables

Veggie Mash

Super-Duper Brownie Pudding Cake

Sticky Toffee Pudding

inty Hot Cocoa

Wrap your hands around a nice hot mug of this yummy cocoa on a frosty morning. It's guaranteed to warm your innards and delight all your senses.

2 cups hot cocoa mix

10 cups water

30 chocolate peppermint patties (such as York brand)

Place all ingredients in slow cooker and stir to combine. Cover and cook on HIGH for 2 hours or on LOW for 3 to 4 hours. Stir and serve.

SERVES: 10

SLOW COOKER SIZE: 4 quart

PREP TIME: 5 minutes

COOKING TIME: 2 hours on HIGH

Serving Suggestions

Serve right out of the slow cooker set on LOW, or pour into a large thermos to keep warm on the table or around the campfire.

Variations

If you don't have a gang to serve, you can make 4 cups at a time in a small 1½-quart slow cooker by using ¾ cup cocoa mix, 4 cups water, and 12 mint patties.

Tip

You can purchase large containers of peppermint patties at discount warehouse stores such as Costco.

Curried Nuts

Do you have guests coming and too much to do at the last minute? Just take 5 minutes to throw these ingredients into your slow cooker and you'll have something a little different to serve with cocktails.

2 tablespoons melted butter

2 tablespoons curry powder

1 teaspoon salt

4 cups mixed nuts

1. Place the butter, curry powder, and salt in the slow cooker. Stir in the mixed nuts to coat well.

2. Cover and cook on HIGH for 2 hours. Serve warm or cool completely and store in an airtight container.

SERVES: 8

SLOW COOKER SIZE: 1½ quart

PREP TIME: 5 minutes

COOKING TIME: 2 hours on HIGH

Serving Suggestions

Serve these flavorful nibbles with your favorite beverage.

Variations

You can change the type of nuts and seasonings to suit your fancy. Try peanuts and various types of chili powders for starters.

Tip

Buy mixed nuts on sale or in large cans at a warehouse discount store to save money. Freeze excess to retain freshness.

nockout Dip

It's a guy thing—what can we say? This dip just knocks 'em out. Set some out at your next get-together and watch the men flock to it. It's a guaranteed hit!

2 pounds hot Italian sausage, casings removed

1 (.6-ounce) package dry Good Seasons Zesty Italian salad dressing mix

2 pounds Kraft Velveeta processed cheese, cut into 1-inch cubes

¾ cup evaporated milk

½ green pepper, finely chopped

1 teaspoon hot sauce such as Tabasco

Tortilla chips

SERVES: 8

SLOW COOKER SIZE: 4 quart

PREP TIME: 40 minutes

COOKING TIME: 2 hours on HIGH

Serving Suggestions

This can be served right from the slow cooker with tortilla chips, sturdy crackers, or assorted vegetables.

Variations

You can lighten this recipe a little by substituting turkey sausage for the Italian sausage, Lite Velveeta cheese, and evaporated skim milk

Tip

If left on LOW for a long time, this dip will thicken up. Just thin out with more evaporated milk, if necessary.

1. In a nonstick skillet over MEDIUM heat, crumble the sausage and cook until well browned, breaking up any large chunks. Remove from heat, drain well, then stir in the packet of salad dressing mix. Pour into slow cooker.

2. Add the rest of the ingredients, except tortilla chips, to the slow cooker and stir to combine. Cover and cook on HIGH for 2 hours, stirring once after 1 hour to blend in the melting cheese.

3. Reduce heat to LOW or WARM and serve right out of the slow cooker with tortilla chips for dipping.

*C*hristmas Morning Baked Apples

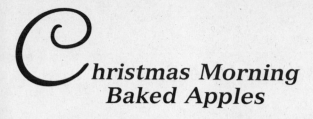

For a super simple breakfast that cooks while Santa's busy delivering toys to all the girls and boys, try these yummy apples served with your favorite coffee cake. Also, we recommend this Web page with a fabulous chart of various apples and their uses: http://www.deliciousorchardsnj.com/doapples.html.

4 slightly tart baking apples, such as Rome, Braburn, Fuji, Jonagold, Northern Spy, Winesap, Golden Delicious, or Granny Smith

½ cup light or dark brown sugar

1 teaspoon cinnamon

1 teaspoon butter, softened

½ cup apple cider

1. Core the apples but do not cut all the way through to the bottom of the apple; leave about ¼ inch of apple at the bottom. Widen the hole to accomodate all the filling.

2. In a small bowl, combine the sugar, cinnamon, and butter with a fork. Evenly spoon some of the mixture into the center of each apple.

3. Pour the cider into the slow cooker pot, then carefully place the filled apples in the pot. Cover and cook on LOW for 4 to 6 hours.

4. With tongs, carefully remove the apples to individual serving bowls

SERVES: 4

SLOW COOKER SIZE: 4 quart

PREP TIME: 15 minutes

COOKING TIME: 4 to 6 hours on LOW

Serving Suggestions

If you prefer, serve these for dessert instead. They're wonderful with a scoop of good vanilla ice cream.

Variations

To the butter/sugar mixture you could also add raisins, nuts, dried cranberries, or chopped dates.

Tip

Try using a melon baller to core the apples—works like a charm.

To cook these overnight, set them in the slow cooker plugged into a light timer set to turn on 4 to 6 hours before you want to serve them.

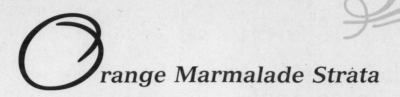

Orange Marmalade Strata

Here's another breakfast dish you can easily start late at night and have ready for breakfast the next morning.

1 tablespoon butter or cooking oil spray

1-pound loaf French or Italian bread, sliced into
½-inch-thick slices

1 (8-ounce) package cream cheese, softened

1 cup orange marmalade

12 eggs

1 cup milk

½ teaspoon salt

2 tablespoons Grand Marnier or 1 tablespoon
orange juice concentrate

Powdered sugar

SERVES: 6

SLOW COOKER SIZE: 4 quart

PREP TIME: 30 minutes

COOKING TIME: 4½ hours on LOW

Serving Suggestions

Serve with a cluster of red grapes or fresh strawberries on the side.

Variations

To lighten this recipe, substitute reduced fat or fat-free cream cheese, 1% milk, and 3 cups of Egg Beaters for the eggs

Tip

To cook overnight, plug the slow cooker into a timer and set to delay the start of cooking for two hours. If you have a slow cooker with a built-in timer, you can do the same thing and also set its switch to WARM when done.

1. Rub or spray the sides and bottom of slow cooker with butter or cooking oil spray.

2. Preheat the broiler. Place the bread slices on 1 or 2 large baking sheets and toast under the broiler until golden brown.

3. Generously spread the softened cream cheese on half of the toast pieces. Then spread marmalade over the cream cheese. Top with the remaining slices of toast. With a sharp knife, cut each into 1-inch cubes and place in the slow cooker.

4. Combine the eggs, milk, salt, and Grand Marnier in a separate bowl and whisk until

well blended. Pour over the toast cubes. Press bread cubes into egg mixture to moisten well. Cover and cook on LOW for 4½ hours.

5. Serve warm with powdered sugar sprinkled on top.

*O*ur Favorite Split Pea Soup

If we don't make this at least once each winter, we feel the season was somehow incomplete. So next time you cook ham, hold onto that ham bone. You'll want to throw it into this soup. It's the perfect warmer-upper on a cold winter night. It's good the day after, too. You'll just need to thin it out with a little hot water.

1 pound dried split peas

7 cups water

1 ham bone with some meat still attached

1 cup chopped onions

1 cup sliced celery (about 2 stalks)

1 cup diced, peeled carrots (about 2 carrots)

1/2 teaspoon dried thyme

1/2 teaspoon dried marjoram

1 pinch red pepper flakes, optional

Salt and pepper to taste

1. Place all ingredients in slow cooker.

2. Cover and cook on LOW heat for 6 to 8 hours, until peas are soft.

3. Remove ham bone and stir soup well to mash peas and thicken soup. If necessary, you can use an immersion blender to fully mash all the split peas.

4. Cut any remaining ham off the bone and dice. Return the ham to the soup. Taste before serving. If necessary, reseason with a dash of salt, pepper, and any other flavors that may have cooked out.

SERVES: 6

SLOW COOKER SIZE: 4 quart

PREP TIME: 10 minutes

COOKING TIME: 6 to 8 hours on LOW

Serving Suggestions

A loaf of homemade rye bread is the perfect companion for this hearty soup. If you have a bread machine, here's one of our favorite rye bread recipes from *Bread Machine Magic*:

1 3/8- to 1 1/2-cups buttermilk
1 1/2 teaspoons salt
1 1/2 tablespoons butter
2 tablespoons brown sugar
3 cups bread flour
1 cup rye flour
1 teaspoon caraway seeds
3 teaspoons yeast
Bake on standard or whole wheat cycle.

Variations

You can substitute 2 pork hocks or precooked smoked sausage for the ham and bone.

Try adding some cauliflower florets for an even heartier soup. Replace the thyme and marjoram with 2 teaspoons cumin.

Omit the ham bone to turn this into a good vegetarian meal.

Tip

Pea and bean soups will usually develop a foam on the top after a few hours or cooking. If you're home, you can skim off that foam, but it's not crucial. It will eventually dissipate.

*T*aco Soup

This hearty bean soup is a lifesaver for the weight watcher. It's high in fiber and low in fat and calories. Make a pot every other week or so, then keep it handy in 2-cup containers in the freezer, for those nights you crave a filling meal without the high calorie cost.

1 (15- or 16-ounce) can chili beans in sauce

1 large onion, chopped

1 (1-ounce) package taco or chili seasoning mix

2 cups frozen corn

1 (14-ounce) can vegetable broth

1 (15-ounce) can kidney beans, rinsed and drained

1 (15-ounce) can pinto beans, rinsed and drained

1 (14.5-ounce) can diced tomatoes with green
  chilies

Chopped cilantro, optional garnish

1. Place chili beans and sauce in slow cooker. Mash well with a potato masher or puree with an immersion blender.

2. Add rest of ingredients to slow cooker. Cover and cook on LOW for 6 to 8 hours.

3. Taste before serving. If necessary, season with salt and pepper. If desired, sprinkle with a little chopped cilantro.

SERVES: 6

SLOW COOKER SIZE: 4 quart

PREP TIME: 10 minutes

COOKING TIME: 6 to 8 hours on LOW

Serving Suggestions

Serve this satisfying soup with low-fat baked tortilla chips and a green salad with mandarin orange sections and thinly sliced red onion, tossed with a fat-free vinaigrette. Take your pick of light desserts from the freezer section of your grocery store.

Variations

Stir in 1 cup of your favorite salsa during the last hour of cooking to thin the soup and give it more zip and tomato flavor.

You can vary the beans. Try substituting black beans, garbanzos, or cannelini for either the kidney or pinto beans.

For a few more calories, garnish each serving with shredded low-fat cheddar cheese, lite sour cream, or a few crumbled tortilla chips. For a meaty flavor, stir in a crumbled veggie-burger patty a few minutes before serving.

Tip

An easy way to slow down your meal and give yourself time to feel full before overindulging is to serve your meals in courses the way they do in restaurants. Start with a healthy soup, salad, or appetizer. Turn off the TV; sit and talk for several minutes before serving the main course. You'll find yourself eating smaller portions of the main course because you've already sated much of your hunger. The unexpected bonus is that you've taken time out of a busy day to relax and savor not just your food but also your family.

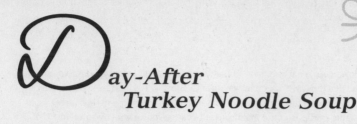Day-After Turkey Noodle Soup

Rather than tossing the turkey carcass into the trash after the big feast, break it up and put all or part into your slow cooker. You'll have the beginning of a two-step, very simple soup. If you're not able to use the carcass immediately, break it up, place it in a large plastic bag, and store it in the freezer for use within the next three months.

STEP ONE:

1 turkey carcass, broken into pieces that will fit in slow cooker

1 onion, peeled and quartered

2 stalks celery with leaves, chopped

1 large carrot, peeled and chopped

5 sprigs parsley

Juice of ½ lemon

Salt and pepper to taste

Enough water to cover ingredients

STEP TWO:

1 (16-ounce) can diced tomatoes, undrained

2 large carrots, peeled and sliced

2 large stalks celery, sliced

1 cup fresh green beans, trimmed and cut into 1-inch pieces

1 onion, chopped

Salt and pepper to taste

1½ cups fettucine noodles or elbow macaroni

2 cups cooked turkey

1. The night before, combine the first 7 ingredients in the slow cooker, including the ½ lemon

---

SERVES: 8

SLOW COOKER SIZE: 4 quart

PREP TIME: 15 minutes total

COOKING TIME: Step 1 cooks 8 to 10 hours on LOW. Step 2 cooks 6 to 8 hours on LOW

Serving Suggestions

Serve with saltine crackers and, later, a sliver of leftover pumpkin pie for dessert.

Variations

You can replace the pasta with cooked rice or beans.

You can substitute chicken for the turkey, including the rotisserie chickens from the market.

This process can be condensed into one day by cooking the step 1 broth on HIGH for 4 hours, cool slightly then strain. Step 2, cook on HIGH 4 hours.

itself. Fill the pot no more than ¾ full with water. Cover and cook on LOW for 8 to 10 hours.

2. The next morning, strain the broth through a fine-mesh sieve into a large bowl. Return approximately 6 cups of the broth to the slow cooker and add tomatoes, carrots, celery, green beans, onion, salt and pepper. Cover and cook on low 6 to 8 hours.

3. Half an hour before serving, stir in the pasta and turkey and heat through. Taste before serving. If necessary, reseason with more salt and pepper.

Tip

If you have more than 6 cups of stock left after step 1, do not discard any of it. Freeze in 1- or 2-cup containers to be used instead of chicken stock in other recipes.

$\mathcal{V}$egetable Chowder

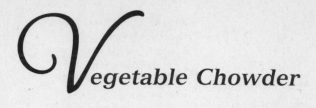

This hearty chowder really fills all the nooks and crannies in your tummy on a cold winter day. And for those watching their weight, definitely try the lighter version we've provided.

3 cups sliced celery

3 cups frozen corn

1 large onion, peeled and chopped

¼ cup diced red pepper

¼ cup diced green pepper

1 (14.5-ounce) can stewed tomatoes, undrained

3 cups water

1 teaspoon salt

½ teaspoon pepper

¼ cup butter or margarine

¼ cup flour

2 cups milk

½ cup (2 ounces) shredded cheddar cheese

1. Place celery, corn, onion, peppers, tomatoes, water, salt and pepper in slow cooker. Cover and cook on LOW for 7 to 9 hours until all the vegetables are tender.

2. In a saucepan, melt the butter over medium heat. Whisk in flour and cook for 2 minutes. Slowly whisk in milk and continue to stir frequently until it comes to a boil. Boil 1 minute. Pour sauce into slow cooker along with the cheese. Stir and continue to cook until the cheese melts.

3. Taste before serving. If necessary, reseason with a dash of salt and pepper.

SERVES: 6
SLOW COOKER SIZE: 4 quart
PREP TIME: 10 minutes
COOKING TIME: 7 to 9 hours on LOW

Serving Suggestions

Serve with a basket of corn muffins and honey butter. A dish of chocolate pudding and a dollop of whipped cream would bring the meal to an end.

Variations

To lighten, omit the butter, flour, milk and cheese and replace with 2 cups of water. Skip step 2 and instead stir in 1¼ to 1½ cups of instant potato flakes at the end to thicken the soup as desired.

Tip

Do you have a friend or relative who is homebound or going through a difficult time? This soup would make a healthy and comforting meal to share with them.

Turkey-and-Dumplings Soup

This recipe converts the previous Day-After Turkey Noodle Soup recipe into a turkey-and-dumplings soup. So save those carcasses!

SOUP:

1 recipe Day-After Turkey Noodle Soup (see page 198)

2 large potatoes, peeled and cut into ½-inch cubes

DUMPLINGS:

1 cup buttermilk baking mix such as Bisquick

⅓ cup milk

2 teaspoons dehydrated chopped onion

1 tablespoon minced fresh parsley or 1 teaspoon dried parsley

1. Follow the recipe for Day-After Turkey Noodle Soup with these exceptions: add the potatoes listed above with the other ingredients in step 2 and omit the noodles.

2. About 1 hour before serving, increase the heat to HIGH. In a bowl, combine the dumpling ingredients and stir just until no longer dry; do not overmix. Drop large heaping spoonfuls of the mixture onto the hot soup. Cover and cook on HIGH about 45 minutes until the dumplings are set and fully cooked.

SERVES: 8	
SLOW COOKER SIZE: 4 quart	
PREP TIME: 5 minutes	
COOKING TIME: 6 to 8 hours on LOW	

Serving Suggestions

The only thing this hearty soup needs as an accompaniment is a sliver of leftover pumpkin pie for dessert.

Variations

You can vary the herbs in the dumplings as desired or omit altogether. For example, we like to substitute ¼ cup cornmeal for ¼ cup of the baking mix and replace the parsley with fresh cilantro.

Tip

To extract the most juice from a lemon, roll it on the countertop first, pressing hard on it as you roll it around.

$\mathcal{G}$ame Day Chowder

This bountiful soup is ideal for a potluck meal, informal get-together, or sports event! The beauty of it is that you can prepare it overnight, and then it will hold for an entire football game on low or warm heat in the slow cooker.

1 tablespoon vegetable oil

1 pound pork or turkey sausage

3 cups water

2 (15-ounce) cans kidney beans, rinsed and drained

1 (28-ounce) can crushed tomatoes in puree

2 cups peeled and diced potato

1 onion, peeled and chopped

1 clove garlic, minced

1½ teaspoons salt

½ teaspoon pepper

½ teaspoon dried basil

¼ teaspoon caraway seeds

1 large pinch of crushed red pepper flakes

½ green bell pepper, seeded and chopped

1. In a large skillet, heat the oil over MEDIUM heat. Crumble and add the sausage to the pan; cook until no longer pink, about 8 minutes. Drain well.

2. Place all ingredients, including the sausage, in slow cooker and stir to combine. Cover and cook on LOW for 8 to 10 hours.

3. Taste before serving. If necessary, reseason with a dash of salt, pepper, and any other flavors that may have been diluted during cooking.

SERVES: 6

SLOW COOKER SIZE: 4 quart

PREP TIME: 20 minutes

COOKING TIME: 8 to 10 hours on LOW

Serving Suggestions

Serve with big, soft bread sticks drizzled with garlic butter.

Variations

For a heartier flavor, substitute 1 cup dry red wine for 1 cup of the water.

Substitute cannelini or green beans for one or both cans of the kidney beans.

Tip

If you choose to cook this overnight to serve the next day for a football game, cook the sausage and add it in the morning.

Crocked Cranberry Sauce

Give yourself a break during the holidays and have the slow cooker take care of the cranberry sauce for you. Just throw everything into the crock and cook it overnight, using a timer to start it about 4 hours before you arise for the day. Better yet, make it several days in advance and keep it in the refrigerator until needed.

2 (12-ounce) bags fresh cranberries

2 cups sugar

1/3 cup orange-flavored liqueur, such as
   Grand Marnier or Cointreau

SERVES: 10

SLOW COOKER SIZE: 4 quart

PREP TIME: 10 minutes

COOKING TIME: 5 hours on LOW

1. Rinse and drain cranberries, removing any small stems. Place all ingredients in slow cooker and stir to combine. Cover and cook on LOW for 4 hours.

2. Remove lid and stir well. Most berries will break up and the sauce will thicken naturally. Taste for sweetness. If too tart for your taste, you can stir in several more tablespoons sugar until desired sweetness is achieved.

3. Replace lid and cook 1 hour more on LOW. Remove lid, turn off heat, and break up any remaining whole berries with a wooden spoon or potato masher. Let sit until room temperature then pour mixture into a serving bowl, cover with plastic wrap, and refrigerate for several hours. This can be made several days in advance.

Serving Suggestions:

If you pour this into a lightly oiled, fluted or shaped mold, it will make a lovely presentation when unmolded.

Variations:

We've tried this with brandy in place of the orange-flavored liqueur and it's equally as good.

You can also substitute a good pulpy orange juice for the liqueur.

Tip

If you place the plastic wrap directly on the surface of the cranberry sauce before refrigerating, it will prevent a skin from forming on top.

$\mathcal{B}$aked Beans from Scratch

You'll need to start these a day ahead or first thing in the morning. They're definitely worth the extra time and effort.

2 (1-pound packages) dry navy beans or small white beans

2 tablespoons oil

1 cup peeled and chopped onion

10 cups water

1 pound thick-sliced bacon, diced

1 cup peeled and coarsely chopped onion

½ cup dark brown sugar

½ cup molasses

2 tablespoons Dijon mustard

2 teaspoons salt

½ teaspoon pepper

1½ cups reserved cooking liquid

1. The night before, or first thing in the morning, pick over the dry beans and remove any debris. Place in a colander and rinse well under running water.

2. Place beans, oil, 1 cup chopped onion, and 10 cups water in slow cooker and stir to combine. Cover and cook on HIGH for 4 hours until the beans are barely tender.

3. Drain beans in a colander and reserve about 2 cups of the cooking liquid. Set aside.

4. Return beans to slow cooker. Gently stir in the bacon and 1 cup coarsely chopped onion.

SERVES: 12

SLOW COOKER SIZE: 6 quart

PREP TIME: 25 minutes total

COOKING TIME: 4 hours on HIGH then 6 to 8 hours on LOW

Serving Suggestions

Serve with steamed brown bread (look for it in cans in the baked bean section of your market), and grilled sausages or weiners.

Variations

Cut this recipe in half for the smaller slow cookers.

For a darker color and a thicker sauce, turn the heat to HIGH after 6 hours and cook, uncovered, 1 hour more. Gently stir once or twice.

You can substitute Canadian bacon or turkey bacon for regular bacon.

Tip

If starting the night before, you can set the slow cooker on a timer to start 4 hours before you plan to arise the next morning.

5. In a separate bowl, combine the brown sugar, molasses, mustard, salt, pepper, and 1½ cups of reserved cooking liquid. Stir; pour over the beans.

6. Cover and cook on LOW 6 to 8 hours, gently stirring occasionally after the first 4 hours.

Chili and Cornbread
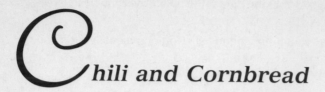

We've cooked countless pots of chili over the years, but this is one of the few recipes that stayed in our recipe files. It was easy to adapt to the slow cooker and we added the cornbread as a topping.

CHILI:

1 tablespoon vegetable oil

3 pounds boneless chuck roast or round steak, trimmed of fat, cut into 1-inch cubes

2 cloves garlic, minced

6 tablespoons chili powder

2 teaspoons ground cumin

$\frac{1}{4}$ teaspoon pepper

3 tablespoons flour

2 cups beef broth or 2 cups water and 2 teaspoons beef broth base or 2 cups water and 2 beef bouillon cubes

2 (15-ounce) cans kidney beans, rinsed and drained

1 teaspoon salt

Sour cream, optional

Peeled and diced avocado, optional

Chopped onion, optional

CORNMEAL TOPPING:

$\frac{1}{2}$ cup all-purpose flour

$\frac{1}{2}$ cup yellow cornmeal

1 teaspoon baking powder

$\frac{1}{2}$ teaspoon salt

2 tablespoons shortening

$\frac{1}{2}$ cup milk

2 tablespoons chopped green Anaheim or jalapeño chiles

SERVES: 6	
SLOW COOKER SIZE: 4 quart	
PREP TIME: 45 minutes total	
COOKING TIME: 6 to 8 hours on LOW	

Serving Suggestions

Cool down your tastebuds with a dish of orange or lemon sherbet for dessert.

Variations

If you prefer more sauce, just stir in 1 cup of warm water or more broth in the beginning or when you add the beans and topping.

You can used fresh chiles in the cornmeal topping or use canned diced green chiles.

To save quite a bit of time, you can substitute 3 pounds stew meat for the roast and omit the topping.

Tip

To brown the meat properly, do it in two or three batches. If the Dutch oven is too crowded, the meat will just steam and not brown properly.

1. In a large Dutch oven, brown the meat in oil over MEDIUM-HIGH heat until no longer pink and most of the liquid has evaporated, about 15 minutes. (If liquid remains, pour it off.) Add the garlic and cook 1 minute more.

2. In a bowl, combine the chili powder, cumin, pepper, and flour. Sprinkle the mixture over the meat and stir.

3. Stir in the beef broth. Bring to a boil and boil for 1 minute, scraping up any brown bits on the bottom of the pan.

4. Pour the beef mixture into slow cooker; cover and cook on LOW for 6 to 8 hours until the meat is tender.

5. About 1¼ hours before serving, make cornmeal topping. Place flour, cornmeal, baking powder, and salt in food processor. Pulse several times until blended. Add shortening and process briefly until mixture is crumbly. Add milk and pulse several more times until combined. Remove blade and stir in chiles. Set aside.

6. Turn slow cooker to HIGH and stir in the kidney beans and salt. Pour cornbread mixture on top, cover and cook on HIGH 1 hour.

7. Taste before serving. If necessary, reseason with a dash of salt, pepper, and any other flavors that may have cooked out.

8. Serve hot in bowls with a dollop of sour cream, diced avocado, and a sprinkle of chopped onions, if desired.

Chicken and Dumplings

This homey stew is a favorite with young and old alike. We love its convenience. For a small investment of time, you'll have everything you need for dinner in one pot: meat, vegetables, and even a "bread."

STEW:

1 large russet potato, peeled and diced

2 large carrots, peeled and diced

¼ pound mushrooms, cleaned and sliced

1 medium onion, chopped

1 large stalk celery, sliced

¾ cup flour

1 teaspoon salt

½ teaspoon pepper

1 teaspoon poultry seasoning

2 pounds boneless, skinless chicken breasts or tenders, cut into bite-size pieces

2 tablespoons olive oil

2 tablespoons butter or margarine

1 (14-ounce) can chicken broth

1 cup frozen peas, thawed

½ to ¾ cup warm water, optional

DUMPLINGS:

2 cups Bisquick baking mix

¾ cup water

2 tablespoons minced fresh parsley or cilantro

1. Place the potato, carrots, mushrooms, onion, and celery in the bottom of the slow cooker.

2. In a shallow dish, combine the flour, salt, pepper, and poultry seasoning. Stir to mix

---

SERVES: 6
SLOW COOKER SIZE: 4 quart
PREP TIME: 30 minutes
COOKING TIME: 6 to 8 hours on LOW

Serving Suggestions

To round out this meal-in-one-pot you could serve wedges of iceberg lettuce drizzled with Thousand Island dressing for a salad and a plate of gingersnap cookies for dessert.

Variations

Substitute 2 tablespoons chopped fresh cilantro or 1 tablespoon minced fresh rosemary for the parsley.

To lighten and speed up the recipe, omit the oil, margarine, and flour and skip steps 2 through 4. Simply add the chicken to the slow cooker first.

Tip

Whenever working with biscuit, dumpling, muffin or pastry, dough, stir in liquid just until dry ingredients have been

well. Dredge the chicken in the flour mixture, shaking off any excess, and set aside. Reserve remaining flour mixture.

3. In a large nonstick skillet over MEDIUM-HIGH heat, melt the butter and oil together. Add chicken and lightly brown, about 7 minutes. Remove chicken with a slotted spoon and place on top of the vegetables in the slow cooker.

4. Whisk remaining flour mixture into juices in skillet and cook over MEDIUM-HIGH heat for one or two minutes. Add the chicken broth; whisk together well. Turn the heat to high and bring to a boil, whisking until gravy is smooth and has thickened. Remove from heat and pour gravy over chicken and vegetables in the pot.

5. Cover and cook on LOW for 6 to 8 hours.

6. About 45 minutes before serving, stir peas into stew. At this time, if the gravy seems too thick, stir in the ½ to ¾ cup warm water. Also, taste the stew. If necessary, reseason with a dash of salt, pepper, and any other flavors that may have cooked out. Cover and turn heat to HIGH.

7. In a bowl, combine the Bisquick, water, and parsley and stir until just combined; do not overmix. Drop six large spoonfuls of dumpling dough on top of the stew. Cover and cook on HIGH 35 to 40 minutes until the dough is fully cooked.

moistened. Do not overmix or the results will be tough and heavy.

Pat's Special Beef Stew

During the holidays, Linda, her husband Dennis, and several other couples decided to rejuvenate the old progressive dinner party idea, kicking it up a notch by renting a limo to take them all from home to home. Her friends Pat and Dave Walters hosted the main course and served this flavorful stew. It was a big hit with everyone, and with Pat's permission we've adapted it for the slow cooker.

4 tablespoons olive oil

1 clove garlic, peeled and minced

2 large onions, quartered and sliced

2½ pounds beef stew meat, cubed

½ cup flour

1½ teaspoons salt

¼ teaspoon pepper

½ cup beef broth

½ cup dry red wine

18 button mushrooms, halved

½ teaspoon dried dill weed

1 (10-ounce) package frozen artichoke hearts or
   1 (8½-ounce) can artichoke hearts, drained and
   cut into bite-size pieces

1 (7.5- or 8-ounce) can refrigerated biscuits

1 tablespoon melted butter

Parmesan cheese, freshly grated

1. In a large nonstick skillet, heat 2 tablespoons oil over MEDIUM heat. Add the onions and sauté until soft, about 3 minutes. Add the garlic and cook 1 minute more. With slotted spoon, remove onions and garlic; place in slow cooker.

SERVES: 6	
SLOW COOKER SIZE: 4 quart	
PREP TIME: 40 minutes	
COOKING TIME: 7 to 8 hours on LOW	

Serving Suggestions

With this special stew, you could serve a green salad with crumbled feta cheese, toasted pine nuts, dried cranberries, and a balsamic vinaigrette. For a light dessert, slice some fresh pears in half and remove cores with a melon baller. Fill the centers with gorgonzola or blue cheese and a sprig of fresh mint. Add a biscotti or two on the side.

Variations

You could substitute ½ cup more beef broth for the wine, if desired.

The biscuit topping in this recipe resembles doughy dumplings. If you prefer a topping of browned, baked

2. Add 2 tablespoons more oil to skillet. Add the meat to the skillet in two batches and cook each batch until no longer pink. With a slotted spoon, remove meat from skillet and add to slow cooker.

3. In a small bowl, combine the flour, salt, and pepper. Whisk the flour mixture into the remaining juices in the skillet. Cook 1 minute and then carefully whisk in the broth and wine. Bring mixture to a boil; boil and stir 1 minute to remove any large lumps. (Small lumps will dissolve during cooking.) Pour over meat in the slow cooker.

4. Add the mushrooms and dill to slow cooker and stir to combine. Cover and cook on LOW for 6 hours.

5. Taste and reseason, if necessary, with a dash of salt, pepper, and dill. Stir in the artichokes. Add the biscuits to the top of the stew, cover and cook on LOW 1 to 2 hours more. Just before serving, brush biscuits with butter and sprinkle with Parmesan cheese.

biscuits, simply transfer the contents of the slow cooker to a shallow casserole, place unbaked biscuits on top and bake in a 425°F oven 10 to 15 minutes until the biscuits are browned. Brush with melted butter and sprinkle Parmesan cheese on top; serve.

Tip

If you used marinated artichokes, don't discard the marinade. Create an antipasto tray the next night by drizzling it over a platter of cherry tomatoes, little bites of mozzarella cheese, salami, olives, and pepperoncini.

$\mathcal{S}$loppy Joes

These sandwiches are still the easiest way to feed a crowd of hungry kids that have gathered at your home on a weekend night. Just leave the pot plugged in on the counter and a basket of buns nearby and watch the food magically disappear.

3 pounds lean ground beef

1 large onion, peeled and chopped

¼ cup flour

½ cup water

1 (12-ounce) jar chili sauce

1 (15-ounce) can tomato sauce

¼ cup dark brown sugar

1 teaspoon salt

2 tablespoons cider vinegar

2 tablespoons Worcestershire sauce

1 tablespoon chili powder, optional

½ green bell pepper, finely chopped, optional

12 hamburger buns

SERVES: 10
SLOW COOKER SIZE: 4 quart
PREP TIME: 30 minutes
COOKING TIME: 4 to 5 hours on LOW

Serving Suggestions

Serve with pickles, potato chips and homemade chocolate chip cookies, of course!

Variations

To lighten, substitute ground turkey for all or part of the ground beef.

Tip

This is also a great dish to take to a potluck supper.

1. In a large Dutch oven over MEDIUM-HIGH heat, cook the ground beef and onion until no pink remains. Drain off fat.

2. Return pan to heat, sprinkle flour over the meat, and cook 1 minute, stirring constantly. Stir in water. Remove from heat and pour mixture into slow cooker.

3. In the same pan, cook the chili sauce, tomato sauce, sugar, salt, vinegar, Worcestershire sauce, and chili powder over MEDIUM-HIGH heat, scraping up any cooked flour on the

bottom of the pan. Bring to a boil and pour mixture over meat in slow cooker. Stir to combine.

4. Cover and cook on LOW for 3 hours. Add green pepper and cook 1 to 2 hours more. Serve hot on hamburger buns. You can leave this in the slow cooker on LOW or WARM for several hours for serving.

loppy Janes

For a lighter version of the traditional Sloppy Joes, try this recipe. Chances are the kids will never know it's actually good for them!

1 tablespoon oil

3 pounds ground turkey

1 large onion, peeled and chopped

1 (15-ounce) can tomato sauce

2 (12-ounce) bottles chili sauce

½ green pepper, finely chopped

2 tablespoons molasses

¼ cup prepared mustard

2 to 3 tablespoons Worcestershire sauce

1 teaspoon salt

1 teaspoon hot pepper sauce such as Tabasco

12 hot dog buns

1. Heat the oil in a large skillet over medium heat. Add the ground turkey and onion, cook until browned, about 7 minutes. Drain off fat.

2. Pour meat mixture into slow cooker along with all the rest of the ingredients except the hot dog buns. Stir to combine.

3. Cover and cook on LOW for 4 to 6 hours. Serve hot on buns.

SERVES: 12

SLOW COOKER SIZE: 4 quart

PREP TIME: 20 minutes

COOKING TIME: 4 to 6 hours on LOW

Serving Suggestions

Serve with pickles, reduced-fat baked potato chips, and fat-free ice cream sandwiches.

Variations

For a slightly different flavor, try different types of mustard.

Tip

When buying ground turkey, look for white meat ground turkey. Ground turkey using the dark meat is higher in fat. In fact, it's almost comparable to using ground beef.

urry Wurst

When Linda and her husband lived in Schwabach, Germany, as newlyweds, there was a little Gasthaus on the backroad to Ansbach known simply as George's. George was Greek but he sure knew how to make the best curry wurst. Linda spent years trying to recreate that dish, and this comes close.

1 (28-ounce) can whole tomatoes, drained and
   crushed
½ cup hearty red wine
1 onion, chopped
1 clove garlic, minced
1 carrot, peeled and chopped
1 tablespoon Worcestershire sauce
1 tablespoon chili powder
1 tablespoon curry powder
½ teaspoon dry mustard
½ teaspoon salt
1 tablespoon vegetable oil or bacon grease
8 bratwurst sausages

SERVES: 6
SLOW COOKER SIZE: 4 quart
PREP TIME: 20 minutes
COOKING TIME: 8 to 10 hours on LOW

Serving Suggestions

Serve with German spaetzle or hot, buttered fettucine noodles and green peas.

Variations

To save time, you could throw the drained tomatoes, onion, garlic, and carrot in the food processor to chop them up. You could also omit browning the wurst first and just place in slow cooker with the spices two hours before serving.

Tip

Bratwurst are the easiest German sausages to find, but you could substitute other varieties of wurst if you're lucky enough to live in a community where you have access to them.

1. Place tomatoes, wine, onion, garlic, carrot, and Worcestershire sauce in slow cooker and stir to combine. Cover and cook on LOW for 6 to 8 hours.

2. Puree sauce with an immersion blender. Stir in chili powder, curry powder, mustard, and salt.

3. In a large skillet, heat the oil or bacon grease over medium heat. Add the wurst and brown on all sides, about 10 minutes. Place in slow cooker, cover and cook on LOW 2 more hours.

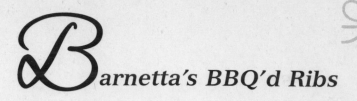

*B*arnetta's BBQ'd Ribs

With her husband Max's help, we tried to recreate our friend Barnetta Hagan's "barbequed" ribs. It was her daughter Marla Bailey who came up with the final piece of the puzzle: to marinate them in honey overnight. All Barnetta's friends used to tease her about her cooking, but no one passed up seconds of these ribs. Her laughter and smiling face are permanently etched in all our memories.

2½ to 3 pounds bone-in pork or beef spareribs

½ cup honey

1 cup barbeque sauce

SERVES: 4
SLOW COOKER SIZE: 4 quart
PREP TIME: 10 minutes
COOKING TIME: 6 to 8 hours on LOW

1. On the concave (back) side of spareribs is a thin, papery membrane that, if left on, makes the ribs a little tougher. To remove, slide the tip of a sharp knife underneath the transparent membrane and lift up one corner. With a towel, gently but firmly tear the film off the ribs and discard. (Or you can ask your butcher to do this for you.) If necessary, trim off any large pieces of fat. Then cut between each rib bone to create individual ribs.

2. Place ribs in a large saucepan, cover with water, and heat to boiling. Reduce heat and simmer 20 minutes.

3. Remove, drain, and place in slow cooker pot. Toss with honey until well coated, cover, and place pot in refrigerator. Marinate overnight.

Serving Suggestions

Serve with carrot-pineapple salad, oven-baked fries, and chocolate pudding for dessert. For the salad, toss together several grated carrots, a small can of well-drained pineapple chunks, a little salt and pepper to taste, and just enough regular or light mayonnaise to moisten.

For the fries, slice several peeled or unpeeled russet potatoes into "fries" and drizzle with a little oil. Heat a large baking sheet in a 450°F oven then add the fries and bake for 30 to 45 minutes until crispy brown.

4. Next morning, place pot in slow cooker, cover, and cook on LOW for 5 to 7 hours. Pour barbeque sauce over ribs, stir to coat well, cover, and cook on LOW at least 1 hour more.

Variations

To speed up the process, omit the parboiling in step 2. However, if you skip this step, you'll need to siphon or pour off most of the fat and juices rendered during cooking before adding the barbeque sauce.

Tip

These are so tender the meat wants to fall off the bone after they've cooked several hours. So take care when stirring in the barbeque sauce.

$\mathcal{S}$weet-and-Sour Pork

You can forego the battered and deep-fried version of this dish by making sweet-and-sour pork, slow cooker style. We think it's every bit as good and much healthier!

1 tablespoon vegetable oil

1 (3-pound) pork shoulder roast, trimmed of fat, cut into 1-inch cubes

1 (20-ounce) can pineapple chunks in their own juice, undrained

1 cup dark corn syrup

½ cup cider vinegar

¼ cup catsup

¼ cup soy sauce

2 cloves garlic, minced

1 large green pepper, cut into ½-inch pieces

3 tablespoons cornstarch

1 cup warm water

Cooked white or brown rice

1. In a large nonstick skillet, heat the oil over MEDIUM-HIGH heat. Stir in the pork and brown on all sides, about 8 minutes.

2. Add the pineapple, corn syrup, vinegar, catsup, soy sauce, and garlic. Bring to a boil.

3. Pour the skillet contents into the slow cooker. Cover and cook on LOW for 4 to 6 hours.

4. Turn heat to HIGH. In a small bowl, whisk together the cornstarch and warm water. Stir

---

SERVES: 6

SLOW COOKER SIZE: 4 quart

PREP TIME: 20 minutes

COOKING TIME: 4½ to 6½ hours on LOW

Serving Suggestions

Serve with a relish tray of raw veggies for starters and lemon bars for dessert.

Have fun with this meal and serve it with chopsticks.

Variations

You could easily substitute 1 pound of chicken for the pork.

To save time (but lose flavor), skip steps 1 and 2 and just place all ingredients in slow cooker without browning the meat first.

Tip

When pouring the heated contents of a skillet into the slow cooker pot, we suggest placing the slow cooker pot in the sink and pouring the contents of the skillet into it there. If you

into the slow cooker along with the green pepper. Cover and cook 30 minutes on HIGH until the sauce has thickened and the green pepper is tender. Serve over rice.

accidently spill, you'll avoid getting burned and clean up will be much easier.

Round Steak Smothered in Onions and Beer

This dish fills the house with such a wonderful aroma! After simmering eight hours in the slow cooker, the round steak becomes fork tender.

2 pounds round steak, trimmed of fat

¹/₄ cup unsalted butter or margarine

4 medium onions, sliced

1¹/₂ teaspoons salt

¹/₂ teaspoon pepper

1 (12-ounce) can or bottle of beer

¹/₄ cup flour, optional

¹/₂ cup water, optional

1. Cut the steak into 6 equal portions.

2. Melt 2 tablespoons butter in a large skillet over medium heat. Brown both sides of the steaks, about 3 minutes per side. (You may need to do these in batches.)

3. Place the remaining 2 tablespoons butter in the bottom of the slow cooker. Scatter the sliced onions on top. Layer the browned steaks over the onions. Season with salt and pepper.

4. Add the beer to the juices in the skillet, bring to a boil, and scrape up any browned bits from the bottom of the pan. Pour juices over steaks in the slow cooker. Cover and cook on LOW for 8 hours.

SERVES: 6

SLOW COOKER SIZE:
4¹/₂ quart

PREP TIME: 20 minutes

COOKING TIME: 8 hours on LOW

Serving Suggestions

Mashed potatoes, gravy, and green beans are the natural accompaniments to this dish.

Variations

You can substitute one (10-ounce) can beef broth for the beer.

In a hurry? Skip the browning step and just place the steaks in the bottom of the slow cooker, with the onions and beer on top.

Tip

Use any beer you like. Darker beers typically have a stronger flavor.

5. If you choose to thicken the juices into gravy, remove the steaks and onions to a serving dish and keep warm. Combine the flour and water in a jar and shake well to blend, or whisk together in a small bowl. Pour the juices into a saucepan, whisk in the flour-water mixture, and bring to a boil over high heat, whisking constantly.

Swiss Steaks and Gravy

Comfort food to be sure! Slow-cooking these normally tough and chewy cube steaks makes them melt-in-your-mouth tender.

3 (.87-ounce) envelopes gravy mix

2½ cups water

2 to 2½ pounds beef cube steaks

½ cup flour

½ teaspoon salt

¼ teaspoon pepper

3 tablespoons butter or margarine

3 tablespoons oil

1 onion, peeled, cut in half then sliced

1 cup celery, sliced ½ inch thick

SERVES: 8

SLOW COOKER SIZE: 4 quart

PREP TIME: 25 minutes

COOKING TIME: 6 to 8 hours on LOW

1. Sprinkle the gravy mix in the bottom of the slow cooker pot. Whisk in water until no lumps remain.

2. Cut cube steaks into 8 serving-size pieces.

3. In a shallow pan or dish, combine the flour, salt, and pepper. Dredge the steaks in the flour mix, shaking off any excess.

4. In a large skillet (preferably cast iron), melt 1 tablespoon each of the butter and oil together over medium heat. Brown 2 or 3 cube steaks for about 2 minutes per side. Remove and set aside. Repeat 2 more times, adding 1 tablespoon each butter and oil to the skillet first.

Serving Suggestions

Creamy mashed potatoes are a must with this dish, although buttered fettucine noodles would work well, too. A wedge of iceberg lettuce with some Thousand Island dressing drizzled on top, steamed peas and carrots, and a chocolate chip cookie for dessert would complete this hearty, soul-warming meal.

Variations

This is one time you really don't want to skip browning the meat to save time.

Tip

If you're lucky enough to inherit a well-seasoned cast-iron skillet, hang onto it. They retain heat extremely well and are prefect for frying and browning food.

5. Place browned steaks in slow cooker; top with sliced onions and celery. Cover and cook on LOW for 6 to 8 hours. If you're home, after 4 hours gently push the onions and celery to the sides of the pot and down into the gravy. If not home during the day, do it a half hour before serving.

6. Gently remove the steaks to a serving platter with a slotted spoon or large spatula and pour the remaining juices into a gravy boat and serve.

$\mathcal{J}$ulie's Chicken

Lois's friend Julie Tyor shared this great recipe with Lois a few years ago. It has become one that her family requests over and over again.

1 (3-to 3½-pound) whole chicken, cut into
    6 or 8 pieces
Salt and pepper to taste
½ cup flour
3 tablespoons vegetable or corn oil
2 tablespoons butter
1 large onion peeled, cut into thick slices
½ pound large mushrooms cut into thick slices
1 can cream of chicken soup, undiluted
3 to 4 tablespoons canned diced jalapeños
⅓ cup dry white wine

SERVES: 6
SLOW COOKER SIZE: 4 quart
PREP TIME: 30 minutes
COOKING TIME: 4 to 6 hours on LOW

Serving Suggestions

Serve this with buttered broccoli; mashed potatoes, rice, or fettucine; and a flavorful sherbet to cut the spice of the jalapeño pepper.

Variations

To save time (but lose flavor), skip steps 1 through 5 and just place all ingredients in slow cooker without browning the chicken first.

You can substitute chicken broth for the wine.

A great variation would be to use canned jalapeños packed in escabeche. This is a Mexican product that adds a wonderful flavor.

1. Wash chicken thoroughly and pat dry with paper towels. Season with salt and pepper to taste.

2. Place flour in a shallow dish or pan. Stir in some salt and pepper. Dredge chicken in flour to coat well. Shake off excess flour.

3. In a large skillet, heat the oil over MEDUM-HIGH heat. Sauté chicken pieces until brown on both sides. Remove and place in slow cooker.

4. Pour off all but one tablespoon of the oil. In the same skillet, melt the butter and add the onions and mushrooms; sauté until soft, about 3 minutes. Pour over chicken.

5. Pour wine into skillet, bring to a boil and scrape up any browned bits on bottom of pan.

6. Pour wine mixture into slow cooker, along with rest of ingredients. Stir to combine. Cover and cook on LOW for 4 to 6 hours.

7. Taste before serving. If necessary, reseason with a dash of salt and pepper.

Tip

If you'd rather not cut up a whole chicken, you can buy a precut whole chicken instead.

Lasagna

This recipe defies the rule that pasta can't be prepared in the slow cooker. In most cases, that's true; but, with the use of no-boil lasagna noodles, this pasta holds up well during the slow cooking process.

1 pound ground beef

1 medium onion, chopped

2 cloves garlic, minced

1 teaspoon salt

¹⁄₂ teaspoon pepper

1 (28-ounce) can whole tomatoes, drained

1 (16-ounce) can tomato sauce

1 (1.5-ounce) package dry spaghetti sauce mix

1 teaspoon dried oregano

1 (8-ounce) box no-boil, oven-ready lasagna
   noodles

2 cups (8 ounces) grated mozzarella cheese

1 cup (8 ounces) part-skim ricotta cheese

¹⁄₂ cup (2 ounces) grated Parmesan cheese

1 cup (4 ounces) grated mozzarella cheese

1. Brown the meat and onion in a large non-stick skillet on MEDIUM heat, about 7 minutes. Reduce the heat and add the garlic, salt, and pepper and cook 1 minute more. Drain off grease.

2. Break up the tomatoes and add to the skillet along with the tomato sauce, spaghetti sauce mix, and dried oregano; combine well. Cook until heated through, then remove from heat.

SERVES: 6

SLOW COOKER SIZE: 4 quart

PREP TIME: 35 minutes

COOKING TIME: 4 to 5 hours on LOW

Serving Suggestions

Green salad and garlic bread complete this meal.

Variations

To save time, substitute 1 large jar of your favorite spaghetti sauce for the tomatoes, tomato sauce, and dry spaghetti sauce mix.

You could also substitute crushed tomatoes in puree for the whole tomatoes and tomato sauce for a less intense tomato flavor.

You could also add layers of spinach, pesto, sliced mushrooms, or various thinly sliced vegetables as desired.

Tip

Crushing the tomatoes with your hands always works, but if you're not a "hand's-on" cook

3. In a large bowl, stir together the 2 cups mozzarella, ricotta cheese, and grated Parmesan.

4. Pour ¼ of the tomato sauce mixture in the bottom of the slow cooker. Break up the noodles to fit the slow cooker, then add ⅓ of them on top of the sauce. Top with ⅓ of the cheese mixture. Repeat layers 2 more times then top with rest of tomato sauce.

5. Cover and cook on LOW for 4 to 5 hours until the sauce is bubbly and the noodles are tender. Top with the remaining 1 cup mozzarella cheese. Cover and cook 10 more minutes until cheese has melted.

6. Taste before serving. If necessary, reseason with a dash of salt, pepper, and any other flavors that may have been diluted during cooking and serve straight from the pot.

you can use an immersion blender to crush them instead.

For more flavor (and more calories), use the whole-milk mozarella and ricotta cheeses.

$\mathcal{S}$avory Bread Stuffing

This is a basic turkey stuffing recipe that can be altered in countless ways. Linda usually doubles this recipe and puts half in the turkey and the remainder in the crockpot to cook all day. Like most people, she has some serious stuffing lovers in the family and can never make enough!

8 cups cubed white bread (about 6 to 7 slices)

8 cups cubed whole wheat bread (about 6 to 7 slices)

1 tablespoon butter or cooking oil spray

³/₄ cup butter or margarine

2 cups peeled and finely chopped onions

³/₄ cup hot water or warm chicken broth

1 tablespoon ground sage

1 teaspoon poultry seasoning

1 teaspoon salt

1 teaspoon freshly ground pepper

4 large stalks celery, sliced

1. The night before, lay out the bread on cookie sheets or an unused table to dry. (You could also dry it in a 200°F oven for one hour.) Once dried, tear each slice into bite-size pieces and place in a very large bowl.

2. Butter or spray the bottom and sides of the slow cooker pot. Set aside.

3. In a skillet, melt ½ cup butter over low heat. Sauté the onions in the butter for approximately 10 minutes until translucent, taking care that the butter and the onions retain their original color.

SERVES: 8

SLOW COOKER SIZE: 4 quart

PREP TIME: 30 minutes

COOKING TIME: 3 to 4 hours on LOW

Serving Suggestions

This is a must with any holiday meal, but it also makes a good side dish for barbecued meats and poultry.

Variations

There are so many ways to vary this recipe. You could add or substitute one or more of the following:

1 tablespoon dried thyme
1 pound cooked and crumbled Italian sausage;
1 can (8 ounces) sliced water chestnuts or toasted walnuts, drained;
2 apples, seeded and diced;
dried cherries, apricots, or cranberries.

Those are just a few ideas. You can also substitute various types of bread.

4. Meanwhile, melt the remaining ½ cup butter in a saucepan with the water or broth over medium heat.

5. Place the bread, sage, poultry seasoning, salt, pepper, and celery in the slow cooker and stir to combine.

6. Add cooked onions; stir. Pour the melted butter and water mixture over all to moisten. Cover and cook on LOW for 3 to 4 hours. Serve warm as a side dish.

Tip

Egg bread is a great base for stuffing. Here's our egg bread recipe from *Bread Machine Magic:*

3/4 to 7/8 cup milk
2 eggs
1½ teaspoons salt
3 tablespoons butter
¼ cup sugar
3 cups bread flour
2 teaspoons yeast

Place all ingredients in bread pan, select the Light Crust setting and press Start.

*T*urkey and Stuffing in a Pot

This is just a no-hassle way to heat up leftover turkey, stuffing, and gravy the day after the big holiday meal.

1 tablespoon butter or cooking oil spray

3 to 4 cups leftover stuffing

About 1 pound leftover sliced turkey, white or dark
    meat, cut into bite-size pieces

2 to 3 cups leftover gravy

1. Butter or spray the bottom and sides of slow cooker pot.

2. Place stuffing in the bottom of the pot. Lay slices of turkey on top and then top all with gravy, spreading evenly.

3. Cover and cook on HIGH for 2½ to 3½ hours, until gravy is hot.

SERVES: 4
SLOW COOKER SIZE: 4 quart
PREP TIME: 15 minutes
COOKING TIME: 2½ to 3½ hours on HIGH

Serving Suggestions

This dish begs for brightly colored vegetables as a side dish: cooked carrots, steamed peas, or butternut squash.

Variations

If you don't have enough turkey, you could chop up what is left and stir it into the stuffing.

If you don't have enough left-over gravy, you could prepare two packets of dry gravy mix.

If you have leftover veggies such as peas and onions, you could stir those into the stuffing as well.

Leftover mashed potatoes (about 3 cups worth) could be spread on top of the turkey.

Tip

To perk up leftover gravy, try adding 2 to 3 tablespoons of madeira wine.

Winter Root Vegetables

This is a good way to cook up many of the seasonal vegetables at one time. If you're not too crazy about one of the vegetables listed, just omit it and substitute a favorite.

2 dark orange sweet potatoes, peeled and cut into
    1-inch chunks

3 carrots, peeled and cut into 1-inch chunks

1 parsnip, peeled and cut into 1-inch chunks

1 turnip, peeled and cut into 1-inch chunks

1 fennel bulb, trimmed and sliced

1 onion, peeled and cut into chunks

6 cloves garlic, peeled and cut in half

2 tablespoons olive oil

1 tablespoon balsamic vinegar

1 teaspoon dried thyme, rosemary, basil, or
    oregano

1 tablespoon grated orange rind

Salt and pepper to taste

1. Place all ingredients in slow cooker and stir to combine. Cover and cook on LOW for 6 to 8 hours.

2. Taste before serving. If necessary, reseason with a dash of salt, pepper, and any other flavors that may have cooked out.

SERVES: 4

SLOW COOKER SIZE: 4 quart

PREP TIME: 20 minutes

COOKING TIME: 6 to 8 hours on LOW

Serving Suggestions

Serve with thin slices of pork tenderloin, quickly grilled or sautéed, and a sliver of lemon cake for dessert.

Variations

For the sweet potatoes, you could substitute 1 small butternut squash, peeled and cut into 1-inch chunks.

Tip

If you're not familiar with parsnips, turnips, or fennel, here are some pointers: parsnips resemble a carrot in shape and are cream colored. Turnips are similar to a giant radish in shape and are usually white with some purple coloring on the top. Fennel is sometimes listed as anise in the supermarket. It's a large bulb with stalks that resemble celery and fronds that look like dill weed. Remove the stalks and fronds and use just the bulb.

$\mathcal{V}$eggie Mash

The next time you serve pot roast and would like to try a side dish slightly different than the standard mashed potatoes, we suggest you experiment with this lively combination of vegetables. It's a very forgiving dish. The vegetables will be tender enough to mash after 8 hours of cooking but will hold in the slow cooker on LOW heat as long as 12 hours.

6 large russet potatoes, peeled and cut into large chunks

3 large carrots, peeled and cut into large chunks

1/2 onion, peeled and chopped

1/4 head of cabbage, finely chopped

1 cup chicken or vegetable broth

1/4 cup butter or margarine

Salt and pepper to taste

1. Place all ingredients in slow cooker and stir to combine. Cover and cook on LOW for 8 to 12 hours until all the vegetables are fork tender. Mash by hand with a potato masher.

2. Taste before serving. If necessary, reseason with a dash of salt and pepper; serve hot.

SERVES: 8

SLOW COOKER SIZE: 4 quart

PREP TIME: 15 minutes

COOKING TIME: 8 to 12 hours on LOW

Serving Suggestions

Serve with a pot roast and a green salad. For dessert, bring out some lemon bars.

Variations

To lighten this dish, use low-fat broth and reduce or eliminate the amount of butter.

Tip

If you peel potatoes in advance, soak them in ice water until you're ready to use them. This will prevent them from discoloring

---

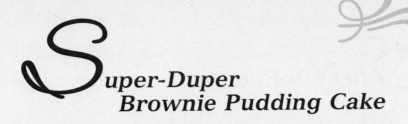

Super-Duper Brownie Pudding Cake

Total decadence. What more can we say?

1 teaspoon butter or cooking oil spray

1 (21-ounce) package brownie mix

1/2 cup water

2 eggs

1/4 cup butter or margarine, melted

1/2 cup chocolate chips

1 1/2 cups water

1 cup sugar

1/4 cup cocoa powder

Ice cream

SERVES: 6
SLOW COOKER SIZE: 4 quart
PREP TIME: 20 minutes
COOKING TIME: 2 to 2 1/2 hours on HIGH

Serving Suggestions

Serve this rich desert with vanilla ice cream or frozen yogurt

Variations

You could substitute mini marshmallows, chopped nuts, vanilla chips, chocolate mint chips, or peanut butter chips for the chocolate chips.

Tip

If you can find it, use Dutch processed cocoa such as Dröste brand for the best flavor.

1. Butter or spray the bottom and sides of the slow cooker pot.

2. In a bowl, combine the brownie mix, eggs, butter, and water. Stir until all dry ingredients have been moistened. Stir in chocolate chips. Pour batter into slow cooker.

3. In a saucepan over MEDIUM heat, combine the water, sugar, and cocoa. Bring to a boil. Pour sauce over batter in slow cooker. Cover and cook on HIGH for 2 to 2 1/2 hours. Serve warm with ice cream on top.

Sticky Toffee Pudding

This very British dessert is gooey, rich, and sinful. But it's not really a pudding, as we "Yanks" think of pudding; it's a sweet, moist cake with a sauce that pushes it way over the top!

1 teaspoon butter or cooking oil spray

CAKE:

2¹/₂ cups dates, pitted and chopped

1¹/₂ teaspoons baking soda

1²/₃ cups boiling water

2 cups dark brown sugar

¹/₂ cup unsalted butter, softened

3 eggs

2 teaspoons vanilla

3¹/₂ cups flour

4 teaspoons baking powder

Pinch of salt

SAUCE:

1¹/₂ cups brown sugar

¹/₂ cup butter

3 cups heavy cream

SERVES: 8

SLOW COOKER SIZE: 4 quart

PREP TIME: 35 minutes

COOKING TIME: 3 to 4 hours on LOW

Serving Suggestions

This is such a rich desert that a little goes a long way. Serve it on a night when dinner was light.

Variations

The sauce can be made ahead—refrigerated until needed, then rewarmed over MEDIUM-LOW heat.

Tip

To chop dates easily, rub blades of scissors with oil and cut up dates with scissors.

1. Butter or spray the bottom and sides of slow cooker with 1 teaspoon butter or some cooking oil spray.

2. In a bowl, combine dates and baking soda. Pour boiling water on top. Set aside.

3. In a separate bowl, cream together the butter and sugar with an electric mixer. Beat in the

eggs one at a time, then stir in date mixture and vanilla. Combine the flour, baking powder, and salt and fold into the date mixture.

4. Place batter in slow cooker. Cover and cook on LOW for 3 to 4 hours until the center has set but is still moist. Serve warm with warm sauce drizzled on top.

5. To make sauce: Just before serving, combine ingredients in a saucepan over MEDIUM heat. Stirring constantly, bring mixture to a boil. Reduce heat and simmer for about 6 minutes, stirring constantly.

$\mathcal{A}$cknowledgments ✌︎

As always, so many friends and neighbors helped us bring this book to fruition.

A big slow cooker hug to Kelly Lockwood, a member of the Rival Crock-Pot family. Kelly really inspired Lois at the Gourmet Products Show and provided her with very useful information on slow cookers.

We'd like to give a special thank you to Judy Self, Lynn Head, Marsha Peterson, Ginger Riggs, Tamera Surovchak, Betty Hamm, Pat Walter, Peggy Ramsey, Max Hagan, Marla Bailey, Julie Tyor, and Debbie Carlson. All of these creative cooks contributed recipes and ideas. Also, we're indebted to Cynthia Buker, Lois's fishmonger, who shared her vast knowledge whenever we had questions.

There were many tasters who helped us evaluate our recipes. The families of George Felipe and Mario Morales sampled countless dishes and always gave us their honest opinions. Mitzi Charlton and her family were eager taste testers, too. Thanks go out to Debbie and Joe Bruni, Dave Walter, and Peggy Ramsey, our late-night bread pudding testers. Linda's coworkers at Bernardo Heights Middle School lent great support and good suggestions. Her daughter Shayna also got involved in the process and offered several helpful comments. But the biggest thanks and hugs go to our husbands Dennis and Jim. With a minimum of complaints, they gave up manning the grills to dine night after night on slow-cooked meals. They were good sports and always offered valuable feedback.

We'd like to thank Marian Lizzi, our wonderful editor, who also helped us with two of our Bread Machine Magic books. Unfortunately, she is no longer at St. Martin's Press, but we wish her the very best in her new career. She has given us a fantastic replacement, Elizabeth Beier. How fortunate we've been to have the very best of editors in all the years we've been with St. Martin's Press!

Recipe Index

C

cabbage
  German-Style Red Cabbage, 175
  Veggie Mash, 232
cakes
  Apple Pudding Cake, 182–183
  Butterscotch Pudding Cake, 86–87
  Lemon Pudding Cake, 132
  Pineapple Upside-down Carrot Cake,
    84–85
  Sticky Toffee Pudding, 234–235
  Super-Duper Brownie Pudding Cake,
    233
Caponata, 139–140
Carnitas, 64
carrots
  Balsamic Glazed Carrots, 126–127
  Hot Pickled Carrots, 34
  Pineapple Upside-down Carrot Cake,
    84–85
  A Pot of Veggies, 124
  Shayna's Copper Pennies, 178
  Veggie Mash, 232
  Winter Root Vegetables, 231
casseroles
  Basic Risotto, 28–29
  Beef-and-Pasta Pot, 122
  Bulgur Pilaf, 123
  Choucroute Garnie, 170–171
  Deep-Dish Dinner, 78
  Enchilada Stack, 72–73
  Ham, Sweet Potatoes, and Onions,
    62
  Lasagna, 226–227
  Risotto Primavera, 74–75
  Savory Bread Stuffing, 228–229
  Slow Cooker "Fried" Rice, 76–77
  Turkey and Stuffing in a Pot, 230
  Viva El Pollo, 120–121
cauliflower
  Cream of Cauliflower Soup,
    146–147
Celia's Freezable Applesauce, 82–83

cheese
  Chili con Queso Dip, 38
  Green Chili Eggs, 95
  Knockout Dip, 190
  Lasagna, 226–227
  Linda's Easy Cheesy Potatoes,
    26–27
  Savory Mashed Potatoes, 80–81
  Slow Cooker Fondue, 154
  Spicy Tortilla Soup, 41
  Viva El Pollo, 120–121
chicken
  Basic Chicken Stock, 8–9
  Chicken and Dumplings, 208–209
  Chicken Curry, 172–173
  Ginger's Five Spice Chicken,
    68–69
  Julie's Chicken, 224–225
  Lemon-Lime Chicken, 119
  Polynesian Chicken, 118
  Poulet Provençal, 65
  Slow-Cooked Jambalaya, 108–109
  Sticky Wings, 36–37
  Viva El Pollo, 120–121
  Workday Chicken and Gravy, 174
  See also turkey
Chicken and Dumplings, 208–209
Chicken Curry, 172–173
chickpeas
  Curried Chickpea Stew, 157
Chili and Cornbread, 206–207
Chili con Queso Dip, 38
chilies
  Chili and Cornbread, 206–207
  Chili con Queso Dip, 38
  Cinco de Mayo Eggs, 40
  Green Chili Eggs, 95
  Lite Turkey Chili, 54–55
  Lentil Chili, 53
  Mom's Chili, 158–159
  Sweet-and-Sour Meatballs, 94
  Taco Soup, 196–197
  Vegetable Chili, 106–107
  See also beans; curries; lentils;
    stews

General Index

Hagan, Barnetta, 216
ham
 cooking time for, 25
Hamm, Betty, 110
Head, Lynn, 133
herbes de Provence, 65
herbs (dried)
 adding to stock, 8
herbs (fresh)
 storing, 44–45
honey
 measuring, 101
hot spots
 dealing with, 3, 143
hot peppers
 handling, 34
household timer
 as recommended accessory, 4
 using, 191, 192
Hungarian paprika
 purchasing sweet, 148

ice cream
 melting, 30
immersion (handheld) blender
 as recommended accessory, 4, 172

kalamata olives
 pitting, 140
kosher hot dogs
 in preference to regular hot dogs, 35

L

lemon juice
 extracting, 201

lid
 lifting too frequently, 3
 lifting to stir, 3
liner
 rotating, 3, 143
 washing, 5

maple syrup
 storing, 96
marinated artichokes
 saving marinade for antipasto, 211
meals
 serving in courses, 197
 transporting 5, 73
measuring spoons and cups
 as recommended accessory, 4
meat
 browning, 3, 94, 206
melon baller
 coring with apples, 155, 191
microplane grater
 as recommended accessory, 4, 92
milk
 adding at end of cooking, 3
 canned evaporated milk as
  substitute, 3
Missy (Lois Conway's dog), 46
mixed nuts
 purchasing, 189
 storing, 189
molasses, 101
mushrooms
 cleaning, 110

N

nonstick skillets
 as recommended accessory, 4
nuts
 purchasing, 189
 storing, 189

O

oatmeal
  substituting instant, 144
oils for stir-frying, 111
onions
  chopping, 53
  freezing chopped, 55

P

parsnips
  purchasing, 231
pasta
  cooking, 122
peaches
  peeling, 100
pepper jack cheese (reduced-fat)
  substitute for, 141
peppercorns
  crushing, 52
peppermint patties
  purchasing, 188
Peterson, Marsha, 63
pizza crusts
  crispy, 19
plums
  purchasing, 133
potatoes
  saving peeled potatoes in ice water,
    232
  sitting overnight, 3
  slicing, 78
  storing sliced, 176
poultry
  sitting overnight, 3, 119
pumpkin
  selecting for purée, 180

R

Ramsey, Peggy, 180
raw poultry
  sitting overnight, 3, 119

recipes
  adjusting for 6–quart cooker, 5
  increasing, xiv
  slow cooker, adapting for, 4–5
red chilies
  shopping for, 93
red wine stains
  cleaning, 138
Rehberg, Bernadette, 105, 160
Rehberg, Dennis, 210, 215
Rehberg, Linda, 58, 78, 106, 120, 148,
    182, 210, 215, 228
Rehberg, Shayna, 92, 178
Riggs, Ginger, 68
risotto
  reheating leftover, 29
Rival Crock-Pots, *xiv*
rubber spatula
  as recommended accessory, 4

S

salt
  lemon as substitute for, 124
sauerkraut
  rinsing, 63
Self, Judy, 22
shallots
  in preference to regular onions, 48
shrimp shells
  saving for stock, 108
skillets
  cast-iron, 222
  nonstick, 4
slow cooker
  adapting own recipes for, 4–5
  convenience of, xi
  cooking tips, 2–3
  dos and don'ts, 3
  and extreme temperature changes,
    5
  overfilling or underfilling, 5
  pouring hot contents into, 46–47,
    114–115, 146, 148–149, 150,
    218–219

recommended accessories, 4
what cooks best, 2
slow cooker meal
transporting 5, 73
sodium
in soy sauce, 69, 118
lemon as substitute for, 124
soy sauce, 69, 118
spices
sauté to retain flavor, 3
spinach
purchasing, 145
spoilage
avoiding, 3
steak
freeze to facilitate cutting, 159
stew
thickening with tapioca, 160
stir-frying
oils for, 111
stock
chicken wing tips, saving for 37
dried herbs, adding to, 8
freezing, 199
leftover vegetables, saving for,
13
shrimp shells, saving for, 108
Surovchak, Tamera, 110
sweet potatoes, 177

T

tapioca
thickening stew with, 160
thyme
stripping fresh, 67
timer
using, 191, 192

tomatoes
crushing, 226–117
tomato paste
in tubes, 106
turkey
purchasing ground turkey, 214
turnips
purchasing, 231
Tyor, Julie, 224

U

unsalted butter, 86

V

vegetables
browning first, 3
leftovers, saving for stock, 13
stir-frying, oils for, 111
round vegetables, cutting, 27
uniform slices, cutting into, 178

W

Walters, Dave, 210
Walters, Pat, 210
whisk
as recommended accessory, 4,58
wine
substitute for, 210

Y

yams, 177